Multicultural Mathematics

Interdisciplinary, Cooperative-Learning Activities

Claudia Zaslavsky

 **J. Weston Walch, Publisher**
Portland, Maine

Users' Guide
to
Walch Reproducible Books

As part of our general effort to provide educational materials which are as practical and economical as possible, we have designated this publication a "reproducible book." The designation means that purchase of the book includes purchase of the right to limited reproduction of all pages on which this symbol appears:

Here is the basic Walch policy: We grant to individual purchasers of this book the right to make sufficient copies of reproducible pages for use by all students of a single teacher. This permission is limited to a single teacher, and does not apply to entire schools or school systems, so institutions purchasing the book should pass the permission on to a single teacher. Copying of the book or its parts for resale is prohibited.

Any questions regarding this policy or requests to purchase further reproduction rights should be addressed to:

Permissions Editor
J. Weston Walch, Publisher
P.O. Box 658
Portland, ME 04104-0658

—*J. Weston Walch, Publisher*

1   2   3   4   5   6   7   8   9   10

ISBN 0-8251-2181-7

Contents

Chapter 2. *(continued)*

Chapter 3. Geometry and Measurement **53**

Reproducible Activities

Chapter 4. Probability, Statistics, and Graphs **77**

Reproducible Activities

Introduction

This book of 58 activities offers something for every student—the gifted and the slow, the eager and the turned off, the advanced and the elementary. Teachers will find it an appropriate supplement and enrichment to the regular mathematics curriculum in the middle and secondary grades. It can also serve as a refresher for teachers of the elementary grades and for adults reentering the academic world.

Today's students must be prepared to face life in the real world of the twenty-first century. Although we cannot predict the kinds of mathematics they will require, particularly with the rapid advances in technology, we can be sure of one thing—they will have to be creative problem solvers. We must help them to attain the critical-thinking skills that they will need for decision making in the future. To be responsible citizens they will have to read a newspaper intelligently, to interpret graphs and statistics, and to seek answers to the challenging questions that arise in a complex world.

Students should be concerned about all people in this "one world" in which we live. Mathematics has always been an integral part of peoples' cultures. Teachers can promote international understanding by exposing students to the mathematical practices of other peoples.

Mathematics is relevant to people's lives in many ways, in areas such as science, social studies, art, and sports. Students should appreciate the fact that mathematics is a living, growing discipline, but one to which even they can contribute.

The activities in this book deal with many areas of mathematics, presented in a way that should arouse curiosity and encourage critical thinking. The content is both interdisciplinary and multicultural. It is designed to make math come alive.

Content of Activities

1. Each activity includes
   - Cultural, historical, or other background information, when appropriate
   - Explanation of the pertinent mathematical concept
   - Problems to be solved, with examples
   - "Think About This" (TAT), an optional section that encourages further exploration of the mathematical concept and of its relevance to real-world situations.

2. Mathematical concepts and skills (see chart on pages *x–xii*)

   Almost every activity involves problem solving and critical thinking, frequently in the context of real-life situations. Additionally, every activity addresses several of the thirteen "Curriculum Standards for Grades 5–8" described in the acclaimed *Curriculum and Evaluation Standards for School*

Mathematics (National Council of Teachers of Mathematics, 1989). These standards are listed in the Concept and Skills Chart (pages *x–xii*), with notations indicating which of these standards are addressed in each activity.

Particular emphasis is placed on estimation, approximation, mental arithmetic, and judging whether the results are reasonable. A person who can arrive at a good estimate of the answer to a quantitative problem shows real understanding, and develops the ability to reject unreasonable answers.

In some activities students are encouraged to use calculators. Research shows that such use has a positive effect on achievement and on attitude to mathematics. A calculator allows the student to analyze and solve problems, instead of getting bogged down in laborious calculations. Moreover, feeding data into a calculator can be a first step toward gaining computer literacy.

3. Connections to nonmathematical areas (see chart on pages *x–xii*)

Many activities deal with topics relating to social studies, language arts, fine arts, and health. Students learn that mathematics has played an important role in societies throughout history and in all parts of the world, from the allocation of grain in ancient Egypt to the allocation of funds in the federal budget of the United States. They become familiar with ancient numeration systems, with the traditional arts of Native American, Asian, African, and European peoples, with styles in home building, and with mathematical recreations of various cultures. The exercises encourage the use of manipulative materials, the construction of models, creative artwork, and other hands-on activities. Students are asked to explain concepts and to justify their conclusions in words, enhancing their communication skills. The Concepts and Skills Chart (pages *x–xii*) indicates which activities involve these nonmathematical topics. The introduction to each chapter lists the necessary preparations and materials for each activity.

Teachers and students are encouraged to go beyond the specific activities suggested in these pages. For example, they might write to an antismoking organization (see Activity 42, Think About This) for literature about becoming actively involved in the elimination of this harmful habit. In every community, environmental problems are crying for action on the part of its citizens. Analysis of the federal budget (Activities 24, 46, 47) might lead to interest in the local education budget. The Bibliography (page 121) lists books and materials that suggest further investigation.

How to Use This Book

1. Most activities are self-contained. For a list of those that form a sequence, see Sequence of Activities, page *xiii*.

2. Activities may be chosen to fit into the regular mathematics curriculum, or to relate to topics in social studies or art. Certain activities may have a special appeal to particular students. Refer to the chart (pages *x–xii*) for the mathematical and nonmathematical content of each activity.

3. Each activity consists of a required section and an optional section called "Think About This" (TAT). The TAT section is designed to stretch the mind and arouse students' curiosity, to encourage creativity, and to increase understanding. It is not necessarily more difficult mathematically. The student may be asked to make up problems and have a classmate solve them, to explain certain concepts, or to carry out research.

4. Cooperative learning. Often two or more heads are better than one. Students should be encouraged to work in pairs or small groups, to brainstorm, to discuss strategies, and to compare solutions. They may find more than one right answer or method of solution for a particular problem. This approach provides students with exposure to real-world problem-solving techniques. If they are not accustomed to classroom teamwork, it may take a few sessions for them to get the hang of it. The results justify the effort.

5. Students may check their answers with the Answer Key (page 123). However, many activities are self-checking. Students develop confidence in their mathematical ability when they know how to take control of their own work and to correct their errors. Here, again, cooperative effort produces good results.

Concepts and Skills Chart

Math Concepts and Skills	1	2	3	4	5	6	7	8	9	10	11	12	13	14	15	16	17	18	19	20
Mathematics as Problem Solving		●	●		●		●	●	●	●	●		●							
Mathematics as Communication	●	●		●			●	●			●		●			●	●			●
Mathematics as Reasoning	●	●		●	●	●	●	●									●			
Mathematical Connections	●	●		●	●	●	●	●	●		●	●	●	●	●	●		●	●	●
Numbers and Number Relationships	●	●		●	●	●	●	●								●				
Number Systems and Number Theory	●	●		●	●	●	●	●				●		●					●	
Computation and Estimation	●	●		●	●		●	●	●	●	●	●	●	●	●	●	●	●	●	●
Patterns and Functions											●				●					
Algebra															●					
Statistics																				
Probability																				
Geometry															●					
Measurement																●				●
Nonmath Subject Areas																				
Art, Construction	●	●					●	●												
Language Arts	●	●	●				●	●		●	●					●	●			
Social Studies	●	●	●	●	●	●	●	●	●	●	●	●	●	●	●	●	●	●	●	●
Health																				

Concepts and Skills Chart *(continued)*

Math Concepts and Skills	21	22	23	24	25	26	27	28	29	30	31	32	33	34	35	36	37	38
Mathematics as Problem Solving		●	●	●	●	●	●	●	●	●	●	●	●	●		●	●	●
Mathematics as Communication	●	●	●				●											●
Mathematics as Reasoning		●	●	●	●	●	●			●							●	●
Mathematical Connections		●	●	●	●	●	●	●	●	●	●	●	●	●	●	●	●	●
Numbers and Number Relationships	●	●	●	●	●	●		●										●
Number Systems and Number Theory																		●
Computation and Estimation		●	●	●	●	●	●	●	●	●	●	●	●	●	●	●	●	
Patterns and Functions								●	●	●	●	●	●	●	●	●		●
Algebra		●	●															●
Statistics	●	●	●															
Probability	●																●	●
Geometry									●	●	●	●	●	●	●	●		
Measurement					●			●	●	●					●	●		

Nonmath Subject Areas	21	22	23	24	25	26	27	28	29	30	31	32	33	34	35	36	37	38
Art, Construction									●		●	●	●	●	●	●		
Language Arts		●	●	●	●	●	●											●
Social Studies	●	●	●	●	●	●	●	●	●	●	●	●	●	●	●	●	●	●
Health																		

Concepts and Skills Chart *(continued)*

Math Concepts and Skills	ACTIVITY																			
	39	40	41	42	43	44	45	46	47	48	49	50	51	52	53	54	55	56	57	58
Mathematics as Problem Solving	•	•	•	•	•	•	•	•	•	•	•	•	•	•	•	•	•	•	•	•
Mathematics as Communication		•	•	•	•	•		•				•	•							
Mathematics as Reasoning	•	•	•	•	•	•	•	•	•	•	•	•	•	•	•	•	•	•	•	•
Mathematical Connections	•	•					•		•				•	•	•	•		•	•	•
Numbers and Number Relationships	•					•	•			•	•		•	•			•			
Number Systems and Number Theory													•							
Computation and Estimation	•	•	•	•	•				•		•	•	•	•						
Patterns and Functions	•								•	•	•	•	•	•		•	•	•	•	•
Algebra	•												•							
Statistics			•	•	•	•	•	•	•											
Probability	•																			
Geometry												•			•	•	•	•	•	•
Measurement		•						•	•											
Nonmath Subject Areas																				
Art, Construction												•			•	•	•	•	•	•
Language Arts		•	•	•	•	•	•	•		•				•			•	•		•
Social Studies	•	•	•	•	•	•	•	•	•	•	•			•	•	•	•	•	•	•
Health			•	•																

Sequence of Activities

Many of the activities are self-contained and can be carried out independently of the others. However, it is advisable that the order indicated below be maintained for the following activities, unless the material has been adequately covered elsewhere.

Sequences

4 and 5

9–11

16 and 17

18 and 19

25 and 26

27 and 28

37–39

41 and 42

48 and 49

50 and 51

55 and 56

16 should precede 17, 22–24, and 44–47.

GRID PAPER

J. Weston Walch, Publisher

ISOMETRIC GRID PAPER

J. Weston Walch, Publisher

CHAPTER 1

Numbers Old and New

Activities 1-15

The activities in this chapter should help students to feel comfortable with numbers. They will learn about the number systems of many cultures, methods of calculating, and relationships among sets of numbers. Students will work with numbers in ways that are different from the usual pencil-and-paper exercises.

The topics in this chapter are:

Activities 1–3: Number words and number symbols in several cultures, ancient and contemporary.

Activities 4–6: Calculating with Egyptian, Roman, and Maya numerals.

Activities 7 & 8: Calculating on the Russian abacus and the Japanese abacus.

Activities 9–11: Fractions in ancient Egypt.

Activities 12–15: Number theory involving zero, prime numbers, casting out nines, and "Pythagorean" triples.

REQUIRED MATERIALS

Activity 3: About 30 toothpicks (or half toothpicks) for each student.

Activities 7 & 8: Materials to make the abacus—beads or buttons, cord, stiff cardboard or Styrofoam®, staples.

Activity 15: Calculators.

Name _____   Date _____

ACTIVITY 1 ▪ Names for Numbers

Have you ever wondered how numbers got their names?

Fourteen means "four and ten." *Add:* four plus ten.

Forty means "four tens." *Multiply:* four times ten.

Eleven means "one left" (after counting all ten fingers). *Add:* one plus ten.

In the English language, number names depend upon grouping by tens. Ten is the *base* of the system of counting.

Write each number in words. Rewrite, using *times* and *plus*. List operations.

	Words	**Explanation**	**Operations**
43	forty-three	four times ten plus three	multiply, add
18			
79			
21			
403			
5060			

In some languages, number names depend upon grouping by twenties. The word *person* in a number name means "twenty."

Rewrite each number name in the words of the English system.

Example: French: *quatre-vingt* = four twenties = _eighty_

1. Mende (Sierra Leone, Africa): *nu gboyongo* = a person = _____

2. Inuit (Eskimo, Alaska): *yuenok tatlemanuk chippluku* = a person, add fingers of right hand = _____

3. French (France): *quatre-vingt-dix* = four twenties, ten = _____

4. Mayan (Mexico): *lahu-yoxkal* = ten from three twenties = _____

5. Gujarati (India): *ogntryss* = one from three tens = _____

6. Yoruba (Nigeria): *aarun din logoji* = five from twenty times two (Remember to multiply before you subtract.) = _____

J. Weston Walch, Publisher

Name _____   Date _____

ACTIVITY 1 ■ *(continued)*

Think about this:

(Work in space below; if you need more space use another sheet.)

1. Why are ten and twenty the most common bases of number systems?

2. Can you count in a language other than English? If you can, write some number words in that language, and describe how they are formed.

   Language: _____

J. Weston Walch, Publisher

Name _____   Date _____

ACTIVITY 2 ▪ All Kinds of Numerals

Nowadays most people throughout the world regard the familiar Indo-Arabic numerals as standard. But in the past, people invented vastly different systems for writing numbers.

1. Finish translating the Roman numerals into standard numerals. Sandy is XIII (13) years old, has II(   ) eyes, XX (   ) fingers and toes, XXVIII (   ) teeth, CCVI (   ) bones, and Ms (   ) of hairs on her head. Her mother's age is XLIV (   ) years.

2. The number *two thousand three hundred sixty-nine* is written in several types of numerals. Study each system. Then complete the table below.

Standard: 2369

Egyptian hieroglyphics: ʔʔ 999 ∩∩∩ ||| / ∩∩∩ ||| / |||

Roman (ancient):   MMCCCLXVIIII

Roman (modern):   MMCCCLXIX

Standard	Egyptian	Roman (Ancient)	Roman (Modern)
54			
	9 ∩∩ |||| / ||||		
			CCIV
		MLXXXX	

3. This is how the Maya people of Mexico and Central America wrote the number 2,369:

   Each dot represents a one.

   Each bar represents a five.

   The bottom group tells how many ones.

   The next group tells how many twenties.

   The top group tells how many times (20 × 20).

   20²: ——— (5 × 400 = 2,000)
   20: ••• (18 × 20 = 360)
   1: •••• (9 × 1 = 9)

J. Weston Walch, Publisher

Name _____   Date _____

ACTIVITY 2 ■ *(continued)*

4. How many separate symbols are needed to write 2,369 in each system?

   Standard _____; Egyptian _____; Roman (ancient) _____;

   Roman (modern) _____; Maya _____.

5. Suppose that the symbols in a numeral were mixed up. In which systems could you still read the number correctly?

   _____

6. Which systems have place value? _____

   _____

Note: Egyptians wrote their numerals from right to left. The number 123 would be written: |||∩∩ 9

Think about this:

Why do most people use standard numerals? Write as many reasons as you can think of. Use another sheet, if necessary.

**Maya calendar symbol
for the third day**

Adapted from M. Closs, Native American Mathematics

J. Weston Walch, Publisher

Name _____   Date _____

ACTIVITY 3 ■ Chinese Stick Numerals

Here is a puzzle. This is a five-digit numeral as written in an eighteenth-century Japanese book. Each digit has the same value as in our system. Read the numeral from left to right.

This is the same number, with each of the five digits written separately. The number is 46,431. Can you figure out the system?

1. These are some of the numerals in the Japanese system. Follow the pattern to fill in the missing numerals in either system.

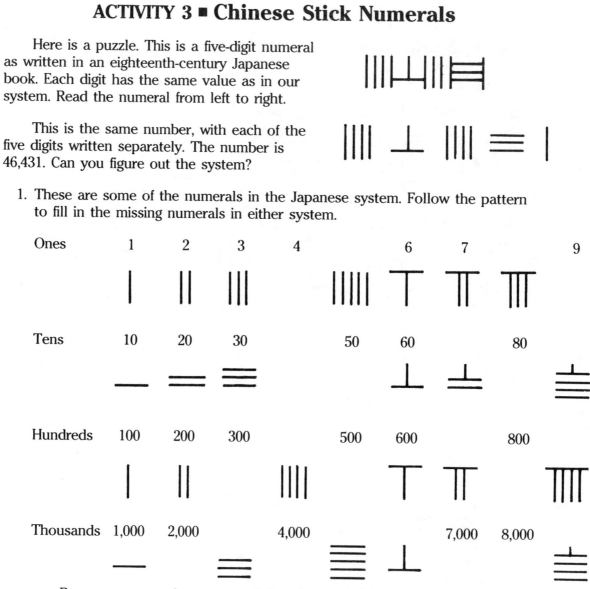

By now you may have guessed that the fourth row looks just like the second row. If there were a fifth row, representing the ten thousands place, it would look exactly like the first and third rows. All the odd-numbered rows are alike, and all the even-numbered rows are alike.

These numerals, called Chinese stick numerals, were used by the Chinese more than 2,000 years ago. Scholars and merchants placed actual sticks on a counting board. The board had columns labeled according to their place value, and people moved the sticks to do calculations. About 14 centuries ago the Japanese adopted this system.

J. Weston Walch, Publisher

Name _____   Date _____

ACTIVITY 3 ■ *(continued)*

2. Write the standard numeral for each of the Chinese stick numerals below. An empty space stands for zero.

	10,000	1,000	100	10	1	Standard numerals
(a)	‖‖	⊥	‖‖	☰			46,431
(b)		☰	Ⅲ	⊥̲	‖‖	_____
(c)	‖‖	—		⊥̲	Ⅱ	_____

3. Have a supply of toothpicks that you can use to form stick numbers. You may want to break them in half. Draw a "counting board" on a large sheet of paper.

   (a) Form the numbers in exercises 2a and 2b with your sticks on the counting board. Then find the sum of the two numbers by combining the sticks in each column. Can you figure out how to regroup the sticks when the sum of a column is more than nine? Write your sum in the spaces below. Then check by adding the standard numerals.

10,000	1,000	100	10	1	Standard numeral
					_____

   (b) Add the numbers in exercises 2a and 2c, following the instructions above. Label the "counting board" below.

					Standard numeral
					_____

   (c) Do the same with numbers in 2b and 2c.

					Standard numeral
					_____

J. Weston Walch, Publisher

Name _____   Date _____

ACTIVITY 3 ■ *(continued)*

4. Write each of the numerals in connected form, like the numeral for 46,431 at the beginning of this activity. In the thirteenth century the Chinese borrowed the numeral for zero from India. This is how the number 3,074 might be written: ≡○⊥|||

   (a) 723   (c) 26,025

   (b) 4,106   (d) 70,308

Think about this:

1. Make two lists. In one list write all the ways in which Chinese stick numerals are like our standard numerals. In another list, write how they are different from standard numerals. You may want to discuss these ideas with your classmates.

2. Work with a group of classmates to compare Chinese stick numerals with Egyptian, Roman, and Maya numerals. Write your conclusions.

J. Weston Walch, Publisher

Name _____   Date _____

ACTIVITY 4 ■ Calculating: Roman, Egyptian, and Maya Style

Centuries ago not many people were able to do more than the simplest arithmetic. They used the abacus, counting boards, or tables of answers. Part of the problem lay in the kinds of numerals they used.

How well can you calculate with ancient numerals?

1. Add in Roman numerals, simplify, and check in standard numerals.

Symbols		
1 = I	10 = X	100 = C
5 = V	50 = L	

Example: XXVIII
+ XII
XXXVIIIII = XXXX = XL = 40

Check: 28
+ 12
40

(a)   LXVII
+ XVII

(b)   CXVI
+ CCIV

2. Subtract in Roman numerals, simplify, and check in standard numerals.

(a)   XXXII
– XI

(b)   LXV
– XXII

3. Add or subtract in Egyptian numerals, simplify, and check in standard numerals.

Example: Subtract. Exchange a heelbone for ten strokes.

Symbols		
1	|	stroke
10	∩	heelbone
100	ϧ	coiled rope

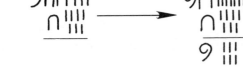

= 106

Check: 123
– 17
106

© 1987, 1993 Claudia Zaslavsky

J. Weston Walch, Publisher

Name _____   Date _____

ACTIVITY 4 ■ *(continued)*

(a) Add

9 ∩∩∩ II
∩∩
9 ∩∩ IIII

(b) Add

9 ∩∩∩ IIII
∩∩∩ IIII
∩∩∩ II

(c) Subtract

9 ∩∩∩∩ II
9 IIII

Note: Egyptians wrote their numerals from right to left. The number 123 would be written: III∩∩9

4. Add in Maya numerals, simplify, and check in standard numerals.

(a) •• + •‗ =

(b) ••••‗ + •••‗ =

Symbols	
1	•
5	—

Think about this:

On a separate sheet, write three problems, one in each system of numerals in this activity. Ask a friend to solve them and to check in standard numerals.

J. Weston Walch, Publisher

Name _____   Date _____

ACTIVITY 5 ■ The Amazing Maya Calendar

Standard numeral

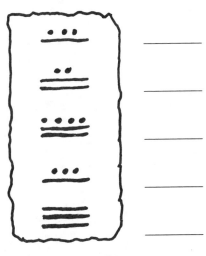

The diagram represents the numbers on a Maya calendar stone found at Tikal, in the tropical rain forest of Guatemala, near the Mexican border. The Maya have lived in southern Mexico and Guatemala for thousands of years. Over 2,000 years ago the Maya and their neighbors devised an accurate calendar. Their year had 18 months of 20 days each, plus 5 additional days, to make 365 days. Each day of the month had a name and a symbol. Some are shown on this page.

Symbol for Day 1*

1. Can you decipher the numbers on this stone? Remember that a dot represents "one" and a bar represents "five." There are five sets of bars and dots. For now, write the standard numeral for each set next to the diagram of the calendar stone. We will come back to it later.

We group our numbers by tens and powers of ten. When we write "237" we mean: $(2 \times 100) + (3 \times 10) + (7 \times 1)$.

The Maya grouped their numbers by twenties and powers of twenty. The smallest value is at the bottom of the column.

2. Write each Maya number in standard form. Show your work.

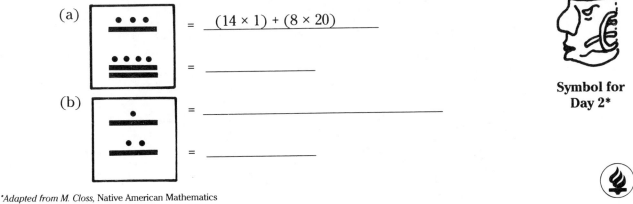

(a)   = $(14 \times 1) + (8 \times 20)$

=   _____

(b)   =   _____

=   _____

Symbol for Day 2*

*Adapted from M. Closs, Native American Mathematics

J. Weston Walch, Publisher

Name _____   Date _____

ACTIVITY 5 ■ *(continued)*

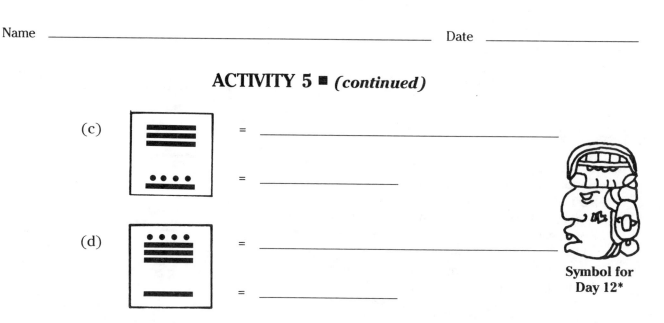

(c)   = _____

       = _____

(d)   = _____

       = _____

Symbol for Day 12*

Here comes the tricky part. The third position from the bottom can be read in two different ways. It all depends upon whether you are reading an ordinary number or a calendar number. Look at the Maya number on the right.

Symbol for Day 15*

As an ordinary number, the meaning is:

$(7 \times 400) + (15 \times 20) + (4 \times 1)$

$= 2{,}800 + 300 + 4 = 3{,}104$

As a *calendar* number, the meaning is:

$(7 \times 360) + (15 \times 20) + (4 \times 1)$

$= 2{,}520 + 300 + 4 = 2{,}824$ days

On a calendar stone: The third position (top) tells the number of 360-day years;
The second position tells the number of 20-day months;
The first (lowest) position tells the number of days.

You can read the date as: "7 years, 15 months, 4 days."

3. Read the following calendar dates in two ways. You may want to use a calculator.

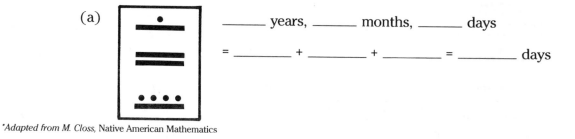

(a)   _____ years, _____ months, _____ days

= _____ + _____ + _____ = _____ days

Adapted from M. Closs, Native American Mathematics

J. Weston Walch, Publisher

Name _____   Date _____

ACTIVITY 5 ■ *(continued)*

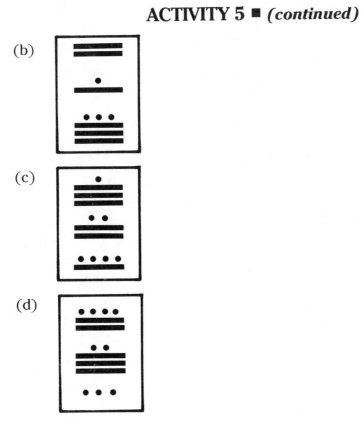

(b)

(c)

(d)

Think about this:

The Maya dated the beginning of their records from a day which we now call August 13, 3114 B.C., over 5,000 years ago. The calendar stone at Tikal tells how many days passed from that date until a certain year. Using your answers to exercise 1, work with a classmate and a calculator to compute the number of days. Then figure out the approximate year of the calendar stone according to our calendar.

This table gives the Maya name and the number of days for each grouping.

Maya name	Number of days
baktun	$20 \times 7{,}200 = 144{,}000$
katun	$20 \times 360 \quad = \quad 7{,}200$
tun	$18 \times 20 \quad = \quad 360$
uinal	$20 \times 1 \quad = \quad 20$
kin	$\times 1 \quad = \quad 1$

Answers: _____ days; the year _____ according to our calendar.

J. Weston Walch, Publisher

Name _____ Date _____

ACTIVITY 6 ■ Ancient Egyptian Multiplication by Doubling

The ancient Egyptians multiplied two numbers by a process called *duplation*, or doubling. A similar method was used by Europeans thousands of years later.

Procedure: Find the product of 6 and 11.

(a) Set up two columns. Write the number 1 in the first column. Write 11, the second factor, in the second column.

(b) Double the numbers in both columns. Stop doubling when the next number in the left column will be greater than 6, the first factor.

(c) Check off the numbers in the left column that add up to 6, the first factor. Check off the corresponding numbers in the right column.

(d) Add the checked numbers in the right column. This sum is the product of 6 and 11.

```
        1              11
     ✓ 2            22 ✓
     ✓ 4            44✓
   _____        _____
TOTALS:  6            66
```

$$6 \times 11 = 66$$

This is how it looks in Egyptian hieroglyphics, except that they usually wrote from right to left:

I	∩I	
✓ II	∩∩II	✓
✓IIII	∩∩∩∩ IIII	✓
III III = 6	∩∩∩ III ∩∩∩ III = 66	

Symbols	
1	I
10	∩
100	ᓂ

J. Weston Walch, Publisher

Name _____   Date _____

ACTIVITY 6 ■ *(continued)*

1. Multiply 7 × 13 by the doubling method, in both standard numerals and Egyptian hieroglyphics.

Standard   **Hieroglyphics**

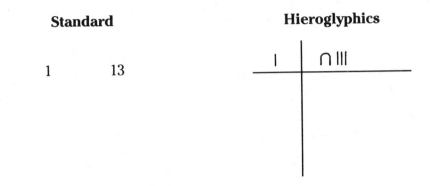

1   13

2. Multiply 11 × 27 by the doubling method. First do the work in Egyptian numerals, and then check in standard numerals.

Hieroglyphics   **Standard**

Think about this:

Make up a multiplication problem in which both factors are two-digit numbers. Find the product by the doubling method in Egyptian numerals and check in standard numerals. You might exchange problems with a classmate. You might also try writing Egyptian numerals from right to left, as they did.

© 1987, 1993 Claudia Zaslavsky   J. Weston Walch, Publisher

Name _____   Date _____

ACTIVITY 7 ■ Counting on the Russian Abacus

If you were to visit a store to buy clothing in China, Japan, or the former Soviet Union, you might see an abacus and a calculator sitting side by side next to the cash register. An abacus consists of several rods on which are placed movable beads. The rods are enclosed in a rectangular frame. For centuries people in these countries have used the abacus for their calculations.

Each country has its own type of abacus. In this activity you will learn about the Russian abacus, called a *scety* (pronounced schaw-tee), from the Russian word that means "to count."

This is a diagram of a simple Russian abacus. The rows are numbered from one to seven so that we can discuss each row. Each row stands for one digit of a number. To show a digit, move the proper number of beads from right to left.

1. Examine the diagram and answer the questions:

   (a) How many beads are on each rod? _____

   How many are dark? _____   How many are light? _____

   (b) The diagram shows the number 427.5. Write the number of the row in which you find each digit:

DIGIT	4	2	7	5
ROW				

   (c) Explain why the third row has only one bead. Should it be moved?

   _____

   (d) Why are the two middle beads a different color from the others?

   _____

J. Weston Walch, Publisher

Name _____   Date _____

ACTIVITY 7 ■ *(continued)*

2. Draw a diagram of the abacus for each number, showing the beads that have been moved to the left.

369.4   2,301.6   5,004.02

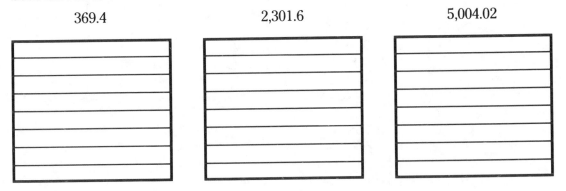

You may have seen counting boards that remind you of the Russian abacus. Boards like those were actually copied from the *scety*. When the French invaded Russia in 1812, a mathematician with the French army saw Russian people using the abacus. He thought it would be a great help to children learning arithmetic. He brought the idea back to France, and from there it spread to other countries.

3. Make a simple Russian abacus having at least three rows of beads. You might string buttons or macaroni on pieces of cord and attach them to stiff cardboard. You may leave out the decimal point row.

4. Think how you might use your abacus to teach a child arithmetic. Discuss with a classmate how to do the following calculations by moving the beads on the abacus. For example, to add 23 + 48, would you first add 20 + 40, or 3 + 8? Try it both ways. Can you find shortcuts?

   (a) 8 + 5   (e) 345 – 42   (h) 6 × 5
   (b) 13 + 9   (f) 172 – 68   (i) 24 ÷ 6
   (c) 523 + 44   (g) 8 × 4   (j) 206 – 99
   (d) 16 + 99

5. Work with several classmates to write a book for children about the abacus. Draw diagrams to explain how they can add, subtract, regroup, and do other calculations on the abacus. Then try it out with children.

Think about this:

Work with several classmates. Make two lists. In one, give several ways in which the abacus helps children to learn arithmetic. In the other, write the disadvantages of calculating with an abacus. Then discuss your lists with the class.

© 1987, 1993 Claudia Zaslavsky   J. Weston Walch, Publisher

Name _____   Date _____

ACTIVITY 8 ▪ Counting on the Japanese Abacus

The Japanese abacus is called a *soroban*. Four or five hundred years ago the Japanese adopted the Chinese abacus, but changed it a bit. The lower rod usually has just four beads, although on some *sorobans* there are five. The upper part of the rod has only one bead.

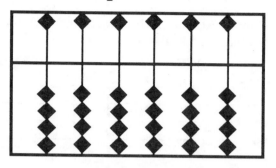

Some years ago a system of finger calculation, called Chisanbop or Finger-math, was popular in the United States. The system was brought to this country by a Korean mathematician. Koreans also use the *soroban*. The finger-calculation system was closely related to that type of abacus.

1. These diagrams tell you how to place the beads to show various numbers. Complete the missing diagrams.

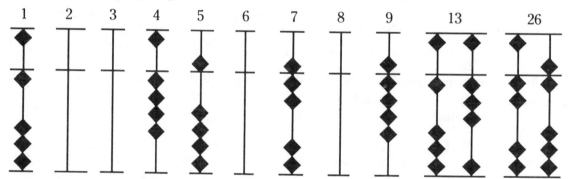

2. Write the number formed by the *soroban* in each diagram:

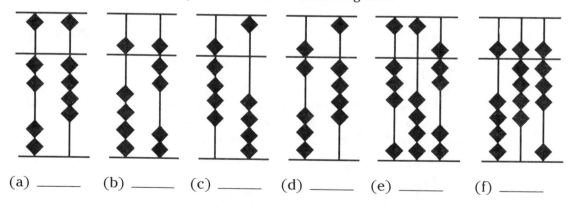

(a) _____   (b) _____   (c) _____   (d) _____   (e) _____   (f) _____

J. Weston Walch, Publisher

Name _____   Date _____

ACTIVITY 8 ■ *(continued)*

3. Draw a *soroban* diagram to show each number:

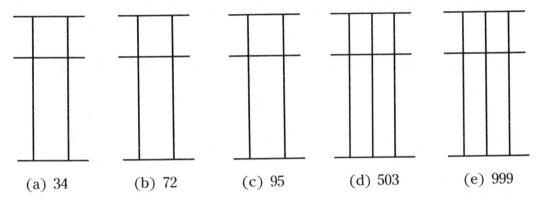

   (a) 34   (b) 72   (c) 95   (d) 503   (e) 999

4. Japanese children learn how to use the abacus when they are very young. Make a Japanese abacus with at least three rods of beads. Use macaroni, beads, buttons, or other suitable materials for the movable beads. String them on cord and attach them to stiff cardboard.

It may seem that working with a *soroban* is slow. But in contests between the *soroban* and the calculator, the abacus was faster for many kinds of calculations. The Japanese learn to do the simpler calculations mentally.

5. Work with a classmate to figure out how to do these calculations on the Japanese abacus. How do you regroup? Try to find shortcuts whenever possible.

   (a) 3 + 4   (f) 31 + 7

   (b) 6 + 5   (g) 24 + 19

   (c) 4 + 7   (h) 9 – 3

   (d) 5 + 9   (i) 14 – 8

   (e) 12 + 3   (j) 48 – 29

Think about this:

Discuss this question with your classmates: Why do you think that Japanese children learn to work with the abacus in school, as well as learn to do arithmetic by paper and pencil methods? Write your conclusions on a separate sheet of paper.

J. Weston Walch, Publisher

Name _____   Date _____

ACTIVITY 9 ■ Fractions in Ancient Egypt (Part 1)

Ancient Egyptian scribes wrote most fractions as the sums of two or more *different* unit fractions. A *unit fraction* has the numerator *one*.

They did not write $\frac{2}{7}$; instead, they wrote $\frac{1}{4} + \frac{1}{28}$.

The scribes had it easy. They had tables in which they could find the answers.

Rewrite as the sum of two different unit fractions, and check.

1. $\frac{2}{5} = \frac{1}{3} +$ _____**?**_____

3. $\frac{2}{9}$

2. $\frac{2}{3}$

To record the measurement of grain, Egyptian scribes used symbols taken from the Eye of Horus.

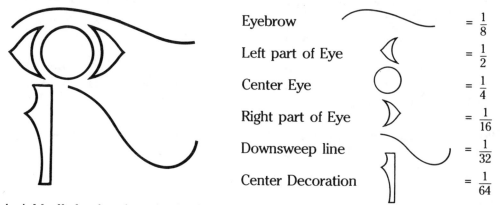

Eyebrow		$= \frac{1}{8}$
Left part of Eye		$= \frac{1}{2}$
Center Eye		$= \frac{1}{4}$
Right part of Eye		$= \frac{1}{16}$
Downsweep line		$= \frac{1}{32}$
Center Decoration		$= \frac{1}{64}$

4. Add all the fractions in the Eye of Horus. Subtract the sum from one.

   What fraction is missing? _____

5. Write the fractions in Eye of Horus symbols:

$\frac{5}{8} = \frac{1}{2} + \frac{1}{8}$

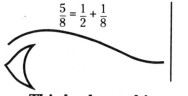

$\frac{3}{4}$

$\frac{3}{8}$

Think about this:

On another sheet, write several fractions having denominators like those in the Eye of Horus fractions. Write them in Eye of Horus symbols.

J. Weston Walch, Publisher

Name _____   Date _____

ACTIVITY 10 ■ Fractions in Ancient Egypt (Part 2): Eye of Horus Fractions

Ancient Egyptians measured grain by the *hekat*, about as much as would fill a container 20 cm high and 17 cm in diameter. They wrote fractions of a hekat in Eye of Horus symbols (see Activity 9).

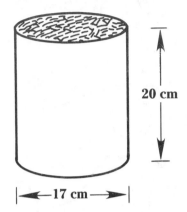

20 cm

|←—17 cm—→|

1. A certain Egyptian scribe recorded the amounts of grain sold to various customers that day. Below are the amounts, in Eye of Horus fractions. (Actually the scribe used a shorthand way of writing them.)

Change each symbol to a standard fraction and find the total amount bought by each customer. Show your work.

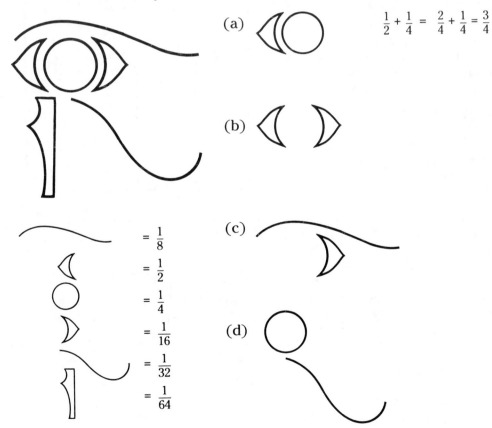

(a) $\frac{1}{2} + \frac{1}{4} = \frac{2}{4} + \frac{1}{4} = \frac{3}{4}$

(b)

$= \frac{1}{8}$

$= \frac{1}{2}$

$= \frac{1}{4}$

$= \frac{1}{16}$

$= \frac{1}{32}$

$= \frac{1}{64}$

(c)

(d)

J. Weston Walch, Publisher

Name _____   Date _____

ACTIVITY 10 ■ *(continued)*

(e)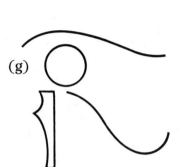

(f)

(g)

2. Here is a neat way to show the meaning of each Eye of Horus fraction. This large square is divided into two equal rectangles. One rectangle is then divided into two equal squares. The process continues until the smallest shape is $\frac{1}{64}$ of the whole square.

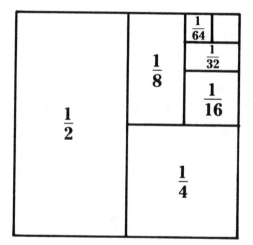

(a) What fraction of the large square is not an Eye of Horus fraction? _____

(b) Notice that only three of the six Eye of Horus rectangles are also squares. What can you say about their denominators?

_____

(c) Suppose you continued to divide the fractions in half and added them. The three dots at the end tell you to continue forever.

$$\frac{1}{2} + \frac{1}{4} + \frac{1}{8} + \frac{1}{16} + \frac{1}{32} + \frac{1}{64} + \frac{1}{128} + \cdots$$

The sum of all the fractions is _____ .

J. Weston Walch, Publisher

Name _____   Date _____

ACTIVITY 10 ■ *(continued)*

(d) This number line shows the addition of the fractions. Write the correct number for each labeled point on the line:

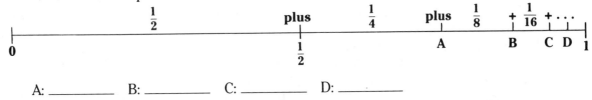

A: _____   B: _____   C: _____   D: _____

Think about this:

1. Look up the story of Horus, the son of gods Isis and Osiris.

2. What do these have in common: Eye of Horus fractions and the Egyptian method of multiplication by doubling? Discuss this with your classmates.

Isis (ASET)

Osiris (ASAR)

Horus (HERU)

Credit: How to Read Hieroglyphics *(Cairo: Lehnert and Landrock Succ., 1974)*

© 1987, 1993 Claudia Zaslavsky   J. Weston Walch, Publisher

Name _____   Date _____

ACTIVITY 11 ▪ Fractions in Ancient Egypt (Part 3): Unit Fractions

The time is about the year 1650 B.C. The Egyptian scribe Ahmose has a big task ahead of him. He must copy on papyrus a very long set of problems, 87 of them, written 200 years before. These problems concern such important matters as paying wages to workers, calculating the amount of grain to make bread, and working out areas and volumes of various objects.

Problem 34, Ahmose Papyrus

Today we are lucky that Ahmose carried out his job. The Ahmose Papyrus (also called the Rhind Mathematical Papyrus) tells us much of what we know about ancient Egyptian mathematics.

Ahmose also wrote a table of fractions having the numerator 2 and odd-numbered denominators from 5 to 101. He probably thought of it as dividing the number two by an odd number. The answer was written as the sum of two or more *different* unit fractions. A unit fraction has the numerator 1.

Here are some examples from the table. Only the denominators are given.

Denominator of 2/n	Denominators of unit fractions		Meaning	Check
5	3	15	2/5 = 1/3 + 1/15	5/15 + 1/15 = 6/15 = 2/5
7	__	28	2/7 = __ + 1/28	_____
11	6	__	_____	_____
23	12	276	_____	_____

1. (a) Examine the table. Fill in the two missing numbers in Ahmose's column of unit fractions. Then complete the third and fourth columns. Of course, these columns were not in the papyrus.

   (b) Why are there no even numbers in the first column? _____

   _____

J. Weston Walch, Publisher

Name _____   Date _____

ACTIVITY 11 ■ *(continued)*

(c) Ahmose used a certain method to find these unit fractions. Analyze the fractions in the table. Can you see the relationships? Use the same relationships to write 2/9 and 2/15 as the sum of unit fractions.

_____

Here are more entries in the table that Ahmose wrote.

Denominator of 2/n	Denominators of unit fractions		Meaning	Check
9	6	18	_____	_____
15	10	30	_____	_____
21	14	42	_____	_____

2. (a) Write the meaning and the check for the three fractions in the table.

(b) Probably you wrote different sums of unit fractions for 2/9 and 2/15 in problem 1(c). The Egyptians liked small numbers. They also liked to have even numbers in the denominators. Why?

_____

(c) Study the relationships between the numbers in the first column and in the second column. Here is a hint: 2/3 = 1/2 + 1/6. When you think you have worked it out, write 2/27 and 2/33 as sums of unit fractions, using the same method.

_____

Think about this:

1. Ahmose wrote 2/25 = 1/15 + 1/75. These denominators are odd numbers. Show the relationship between these numbers and a different fraction in the tables above. Then write 2/25 in another way as the sum of two unit fractions.

2. Discuss with several classmates the different methods that the Egyptians used to write a fraction with numerator 2 as the sum of unit fractions. Then write about these methods so that other students can follow them. If you work in a group, each person might write about a different method, giving examples.

J. Weston Walch, Publisher

Name _____   Date _____

ACTIVITY 12 ■ Is Zero Anything?

Most ancient number systems had no symbol for zero. They didn't need it. The zero symbol that we use today was invented in India many centuries ago. The Arabs, who were great travelers, introduced it to other parts of the world, along with the Indo-Arabic number system that most people use nowadays.

The Maya, who live in Mexico and Central America, invented a different symbol for zero, even earlier than the Hindu invention. The Maya symbol looks like a shell:

When is zero necessary? Cross out the zero in the number 207 → 2̸0̸7 → 27. The number 27 has a different value than 207. In the number 2.70, the zero shows that the number is accurate to the hundredth place. In both these numbers, the zero is necessary. Sometimes zero is helpful, but not necessary. The zero in $0.27 warns you about the decimal point.

Sometimes zero is neither necessary nor helpful in reading the number. This odometer has registered 27 miles:

0	0	0	2	7

The chart on the next page contains a list of three-digit numbers. Follow the directions to fill in each column.

Column A. Write each number in words.

Column B. Rewrite each number in symbols, but omit the zero.

Column C. Write the new number in words.

Column D. Compare the number names in columns A and C. For each number, write one of the symbols:

N—Zero is necessary.

H—Zero is helpful, but not necessary.

U—Zero is not necessary and not helpful.

                    J. Weston Walch, Publisher

Name _____   Date _____

ACTIVITY 12 ■ *(continued)*

	A	B	C	D
340	three hundred forty	34	thirty-four	N
3.40				
0.34				
304				
03.4				
.034				
034				
.340				
34.0				

Think about this:

1. Use the four digits 2, 5, 0, 0 to write two numbers in which

   (a) both zeros are necessary: _____

   _____

   (b) one zero is necessary, while the other is merely helpful:

   _____

   _____

   (c) one zero is necessary and the other is unnecessary:

   _____

   _____

2. Why is a zero unnecessary in the system of Roman numerals?

J. Weston Walch, Publisher

Name _____   Date _____

ACTIVITY 13 ■ Casting Out Nines

One way to check the accuracy of your work is to "cast out nines." This method was known to the Arabs over a thousand years ago. For each number, find the sum of the digits. Then find the sum of those digits. Repeat the process until the final sum is less than 10. If the sum is 9, change it to 0. This final number is called the *digital.*

This is how it works in addition, subtraction, and multiplication:

Addition:
```
      25 ─────────────────────→    7
     179 ──────→ 17 ───────────→    8
   + 892 ──────→ 19 ──→ 10 ──→   + 1
    1096 ──────→ 16 → [7]         16 → [7]
```

The digital of the sum is 7. The digital of the sum of the digitals is also 7. Since both digitals are 7, the addition seems to be correct.

Subtraction:
```
    3805 ─────────→ 16 ─────────────→   7
   – 637 ─────────→ 16 ─────────────→ – 7
    3168 ─────────→ 18 → 9 ─────→ [0]   [0]
```

The digital of the difference is 0. The difference of the digitals is 0. The answer seems to be correct.

Multiplication:
```
     275 ─────────→ 14 ─────→   5
    × 24 ─────────────────────→ × 6
    6600 → 12 ─────→ [3]        30 ─────→ [3]
```

The digital of the product is 3. The digital of the product of the digitals is 3. The answer seems to be correct.

J. Weston Walch, Publisher

Name _____   Date _____

ACTIVITY 13 ■ *(continued)*

1. Find the answer, and check by casting out nines.

Add: Subtract: Multiply:

257 $\longrightarrow$ 7024 $\longrightarrow$ 85 $\longrightarrow$

743 $\longrightarrow$ – 641 $\longrightarrow$ × 36 $\longrightarrow$

+ 1689 $\longrightarrow$ $\longrightarrow$

$\longrightarrow$

Digital: _____   _____   _____

2. Check the answers by casting out nines. Try to calculate the digitals mentally. If the answer is incorrect, find the correct answer and check it. Work on another sheet.

(a)   372   (b)   3804   (c)   82   (d)   426
          528   – 706   × 57   × 93
        + 1756   3102   5574   38,618
          2656

Correct digital: (a) _____ (b) _____ (c) _____ (d) _____

Correct answer: (a) _____ (b) _____ (c) _____ (d) _____

Think about this:

1. Look at exercise 2(c). Does the answer seem to be correct? Actually, it is *not* correct. Find the correct answer and its digital.

    Answer: _____   Digital: _____

2. Why doesn't "casting out nines" work in the case of exercise 2(c)?

J. Weston Walch, Publisher

Name _____   Date _____

ACTIVITY 14 ■ More About Numbers: Goldbach's Conjecture

Back in the year 1742 a mathematician named Goldbach stated his theory:

Every even number larger than 2 can be written as the sum of two prime numbers.

Example: 14 = 3 + 11 or 7 + 7

The number 14 can be written as the sum of two primes in two different ways.

No one has been able to prove Goldbach's theory, called "Goldbach's conjecture," although it has been true for every even number tested. Since there is an infinite number of even numbers, it is not possible to test *all* even numbers.

1. List all the prime numbers less than 20. A prime number has no factors except one and itself. The smallest prime number is 2. The number 1 is not considered a prime number.

   Prime numbers: ___2, 3,_____

2. Write each even number as the sum of two prime numbers in as many ways as you can.

Even numbers	Number of ways
4 = 2 + 2	1
6	
8	
10	
12	
14 = 7 + 7 or 3 + 11	2
16	
18	
20	

                                                    J. Weston Walch, Publisher

Name _____   Date _____

ACTIVITY 14 ■ *(continued)*

3. Why is 2 *not* an addend, except in 4 = 2 + 2?

Think about this:

Continue by writing the even numbers 22, 24, 26, and so on, as the sum of two prime numbers in as many ways as possible. Use another sheet of paper, if necessary. Is there a pattern in the number of ways?

J. Weston Walch, Publisher

Name _____   Date _____

ACTIVITY 15 ■ Pythagorean Triples

The Greek mathematician Pythagoras lived 2,500 years ago in southern Italy. Like many Greek scholars, he had studied in Egypt. Upon returning from his travels, he founded the famous school that bears his name.

The members of the school were especially interested in discovering how whole numbers were related to one another. You may know the Pythagorean theorem for right triangles: $a^2 + b^2 = c^2$. The numbers a, b, c are called *Pythagorean triples*.

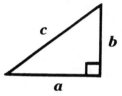

Find the length of the third side of each triangle. Draw and label a right triangle for each exercise.

1. $a = 3$ cm, $b = 4$ cm. Find c.   2. $a = 8$ ft, $c = 10$ ft. Find b.

Examine this table of Pythagorean triples.

a	b	c	$a^2 + b^2 \overset{?}{=} c^2$
3	4	5	
5	12	13	
7	24	25	

J. Weston Walch, Publisher

Name _____   Date _____

ACTIVITY 15 ■ *(continued)*

3. Check that each triple satisfies the sentence: $a^2 + b^2 = c^2$

4. The numbers a, b, c are related in another way. Try to find the pattern, and then write at least three more lines in the table.

   Hints: What type of number is a? _____

   How are b and c related? _____

   Add b and c. How is the sum related to a? _____

Think about this:

1. Long before the time of Pythagoras, almost 4,000 years ago, the Babylonians were writing tables of Pythagorean triples on clay tablets. Here are several lines from a tablet. Check with a calculator that $a^2 + b^2 = c^2$ in each case.

a	b	c	a^2 + $b^2 \stackrel{?}{=} c^2$
60	45	75	
72	65	97	
3456	3367	4825	

2. Find a triple of one-digit numbers that describes a triangle similar to that of the Babylonian triple: 60, 45, 75. How do you know that the two triangles are similar; that is, they have the same shape but different size?

J. Weston Walch, Publisher

CHAPTER 2

Using Numbers in Real Life

Activities 16-24

Numbers are all around us. We need them for shopping, for sports, for making it in school and in the world. In this chapter students will practice mental arithmetic. They will simplify big numbers so that they are easy to deal with. Students will estimate answers to problems and decide whether the estimate is close to the exact answer. If they have not had much practice with estimation, their answers may be far from the exact answers at first. But, with experience, their skills will improve. Some real-world examples will give them the opportunity to use these skills.

The topics in this chapter are:

Activities 16 & 17: Exact and approximate numbers in real life.

Activities 18 & 19: Mental arithmetic applications to West African cowrie currency.

Activity 20: Tom Fuller, African-American slave recognized as a calculating genius.

Activities 21–24: Applications to natural phenomena, population growth, and the federal budget.

REQUIRED MATERIALS

Activities 19, 20, 22–24: Calculators (optional).

Activities 17, 22–24: Almanac or other reference book.

Name _____   Date _____

ACTIVITY 16 ▪ Rounding Numbers

Often it is not convenient or not necessary to use an exact number. An approximate number will do as well, and is easier to work with. Write three different approximations to each exact number.

	(1) Exact number	(2) Nearest hundred	(3) Nearest thousand	(4) Two significant figures
	349,621	349,600	350,000	350,000
	483,450	483,500	483,000	480,000
	24,389			
	158,460			
	29,642			
	983			
	300,206			
Sums				

Find the exact sum of the last *five* numbers in each column. Calculate the difference between the sums in:

Columns 1 and 2: _____   Columns 1 and 3: _____   Columns 1 and 4: _____

Which difference is largest? _____

How do you know whether a number is exact or approximate? An exact number is usually obtained by counting. An approximate number is obtained by measuring, by estimating, or by rounding.

J. Weston Walch, Publisher

Name _____   Date _____

ACTIVITY 16 ■ *(continued)*

Decide whether each number is exact (E) or approximate (A). Write E or A in each blank space.

_____ 1. Thirty-two students were in class today.

_____ 2. The population of New York City is seven million.

_____ 3. Joe is 68 inches tall.

_____ 4. There are 12 inches in a foot and 3 feet in a yard.

_____ 5. About 40 people came to the gym.

_____ 6. In some languages of West Africa the word for *twenty* means "one whole person," and refers to the 20 fingers and toes.

_____ 7. The temperature at noon was 38.4 degrees.

_____ 8. Safe drinking water is not available to 1,200,000,000 people.

Think about this:

Find an article or a selection from a social studies book which contains at least five numbers. Copy each sentence or clause that includes a number. Decide whether each number is exact or approximate, and give a reason in each case.

J. Weston Walch, Publisher

Name _____   Date _____

ACTIVITY 17 ▪ Big Numbers and Approximation

In a TV program about the human body, the narrator stated that there are fifty thousand billion cells in the human body. Of course, this number is not exact. For one thing, it is impossible to count all the cells. Besides, it would bore the audience to have to listen to a long string of words that express just one number.

Suppose that you are writing a script for a television announcer who will read the election results below. Write out in words an approximate number for each figure in the table.

National Election			**State Election**	
Smith	32,368,197			
Chen	15,172,803		Bilsky	1,275,691
Lopez	14,232,169		Perone	498,609
Rodman	1,029,320		Jones	20,142
Total Votes Cast	62,802,489		Total Votes Cast	1,794,442

APPROXIMATE NUMBER OF VOTES		
	Numerals	**Words**
National		
Smith	32,000,0000	thirty-two million
Chen		
Lopez		
Rodman		
TOTAL		
State		
Bilsky		
Perone		
Jones		
TOTAL		

J. Weston Walch, Publisher

Name _____   Date _____

ACTIVITY 17 ■ *(continued)*

Four possible methods of rounding numbers are

1. nearest million
2. nearest hundred thousand

3. nearest ten thousand
4. two significant figures

Which of these methods would be appropriate for each set of votes?

National election: _____ .   State election: _____ . Explain why.

Think about this:

1. Add the *approximate* number of votes cast in the national election. Do the same for the state election. Do these sums agree with the approximate figure for the total in each case? If not, explain why not.

2. Write a script for a television announcer to describe an actual election for a national or state office. You may use an almanac or other reference. Include approximate numbers.

J. Weston Walch, Publisher

Name _____   Date _____

ACTIVITY 18 ■ Mental Arithmetic (Part 1): Money in West Africa

In the past many people had little or no formal schooling. Even today, almost one-third of the adults in the world cannot read or write. Yet some of these people learn to do complicated calculations in their heads. The market women of West Africa are a good example.

A century or more ago, in parts of West Africa, cowrie shells were used as money. Forty shells were strung to form a sort of necklace called a "string."

This table gives the different units of shell money. Calculate mentally the number of shells in each unit. Be sure that your calculation ends with 20,000 shells in a bag.

Units	Number of shells
String	40
Bunch = 5 strings	
Head = 10 bunches	
Bag = 10 heads	20,000

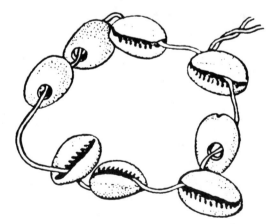

String of cowrie shells

Credit: C. Zaslavsky, Africa Counts

J. Weston Walch, Publisher

Name _____   Date _____

ACTIVITY 18 ■ *(continued)*

Women usually operated the markets in parts of West Africa. In a certain market, women sold the items in the chart below.

1. Calculate *mentally* the number of shells paid for each purchase.

2. Calculate the cost on another sheet of paper, showing all work, and write that answer.

3. Compare the two sets of answers. Check those that agree.

    Find the errors if the answers do not agree.

	Item	Price	Mental arithmetic	Written arithmetic	Agree?
1	Chicken	4 strings, 15 shells			
2	Two mats	1 bunch, 2 strings, 10 shells			
3	Goat	8 bunches, 3 strings, 10 shells			
4	Yams	2 heads, 3 bunches, 1 string, 25 shells			
5	Herd of goats	6 heads, 5 bunches, 3 strings			
6	Household goods	1 bag, 7 heads, 4 bunches, 3 strings			

Think about this:

In Africa today 14,000 children die every day of hunger and hunger-related causes. Calculate mentally approximately how many African children die:

in a week _____ ;

in a year _____

Check your figure for a year by multiplying 365 × 14,000:

_____

Was your approximation a reasonable one?

_____

J. Weston Walch, Publisher

Name _____   Date _____

ACTIVITY 19 ■ Mental Arithmetic (Part 2): More Cowrie Shells

Throughout history people often liked the kind of money that they could also use for other purposes. Cowrie shells and beads, for example, were very good decorative materials. Many games were played with cowries as game pieces. What can you do with a dollar bill besides spend it? Cowrie shells may have been the first kind of money. Loads of them were found in ancient Egyptian and Chinese graves.

People in West Africa used cowrie shell money for many centuries. Foreign visitors were amazed to find that African merchants, both men and women, could do all the necessary arithmetic mentally. They could remember their sales figures and accounts for years.

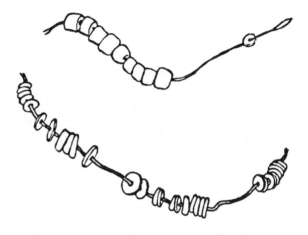

Currency—Beads, Ivory Disks

Credit: C. Zaslavsky, Africa Counts

You can try your own ability to do math in your head. Don't be discouraged if it seems hard at first. People need lots of practice to develop this skill. Just keep at it, and practice whenever you have a chance.

How to play: Work with a partner. First read the question. Then one of you will do the calculations mentally, while the other works with a calculator or paper and pencil (or both). For the next question, change places. Don't try to rush. This is not a speed test.

The table in Activity 18 giving the different units of shell money is repeated here. Fill in the missing numbers, and check.

Units	Equivalent	Number of shells
String		
Bunch	5 strings	200
Head	10 bunches	
Bag	____ heads	20,000

J. Weston Walch, Publisher

Name _____ Date _____

ACTIVITY 19 ■ *(continued)*

1. It was recorded that the King of Dahomey was beaten by the Yoruba (of Nigeria) with a loss of "two heads, twenty strings, and twenty" soldiers. How many soldiers did he lose? _____ (You won't find Dahomey on a modern map of Africa. The name of the country is now Benin.)

2. A certain trader kept her accounts in her head. At the end of one week she had collected 10 bunches, 25 strings, and 128 shells. The following week she received 6 bunches, 20 strings, and 320 shells. How many shells did she receive the first week? _____ ; the second week? _____

In another part of West Africa these cowrie units were in use about 200 years ago. Fill in the missing numbers. Then use this table to play the game described below with a partner.

Units	Number of shells	Equivalent units
String	40	
Hen	200	_____ strings
Ackey	1,000	_____ hens
Head	4,000	_____ ackeys
Sack	16,000	_____ heads

How to play: Take turns filling in the numbers for the cost of each purchase. Then take turns calculating the total number of cowries in your head, while your partner checks with a calculator or pencil and paper (or both).

3.

Item	Price	Total cowries
Two pots	_____ hens, _____ strings, _____ shells	
Three mats	_____ ackeys, _____ hens, _____ strings	
Basket of yams	_____ ackeys, _____ strings, _____ shells	
Herd of cattle	_____ sacks, _____ heads, _____ ackeys	

Think about this:

At the time they were conquered by the Spanish conquistadores in 1519, the Aztecs of Mexico were using cocoa beans as currency; 8,000 beans were equal to one bag. Discuss these questions with your classmates and write your conclusions.

1. Compare the Aztec bag of cocoa beans with the bag or sack of cowries in West Africa in as many different ways as you can.

2. The Aztec number system, like the Maya system, was based on groups of twenty. How is this fact related to the number of 8,000? (See Activity 2.)

3. Research wampum of the northeast Native Americans. How were these shell beads used, besides for trade?

J. Weston Walch, Publisher

Name _____ Date _____

ACTIVITY 20 ▪ Mental Arithmetic (Part 3): African Genius

Thomas Fuller was a remarkable mental calculator. Although, as a slave, he was not allowed to learn to read or write, he was able to do very long and complicated calculations in his head. For example, he could multiply two nine-digit numbers.

Fuller was born in Africa in 1710, and was brought to America in slavery at the age of 14. His fame as a calculator spread across the colonies. He came to the attention of members of the society to abolish slavery. In 1780 two men from the society came to test him. They wanted to tell the British antislavery society about his skill in mathematics.

One man asked Fuller how many seconds a man has lived, who is 70 years, 17 days, and 12 hours old. It took him one and a half minutes to give the answer: 2,210,500,800 seconds. Meanwhile the man was working it out on paper and got a smaller answer. When he told Fuller that his result was wrong, the old man reminded him that he had forgotten to count the leap years. As it turned out, Fuller's answer was correct.

An article in a Boston newspaper noted his death in 1790. The article had the headline: "Died—Negro Tom, the famous African Calculator, aged 80 years."

1. Test your own powers of mental arithmetic by trying these problems.
   If the numbers are too hard to work with, make an estimate. Don't be afraid to keep trying, even if you make many mistakes.

   • Calculate mentally and write your answer.

   • Work out the problem on another sheet of paper, showing all work, and write that answer.

   • Compare the two answers. Do they agree? If not, are they close? If the difference is large, try to find your errors.

Calculate	Mental arithmetic	Written arithmetic	Close or agree?
(a) Number of minutes in a day			
(b) Number of hours in a week			
(c) Number of minutes in a week			
(d) Number of hours in a year			
(e) Number of minutes in a year			

J. Weston Walch, Publisher

Name _____   Date _____

ACTIVITY 20 ▪ *(continued)*

Do you wonder how Thomas Fuller got his answers?

Tom Fuller loved numbers. He could calculate how many shingles were needed to cover a house. He knew the number of seeds to plant in a field. He was an important man to have on a farm.

2. Try to estimate these measurements. Then measure to check your estimate. If the two numbers are very different, try to find your errors. You might work with a partner.

	Estimate	Measure	Agree?
(a) Length of your arm from shoulder to fingtertip			
(b) Length of your leg from knee to heel			
(c) Length and width of this sheet of paper			
(d) Length and width of your desk or table			
(e) Length and width of the classroom door			
(f) Another object (name it)			

Think about this:

Many people of African origin fought in the Civil War. About 186,000 black soldiers served in the Union army. Of these, 38,000 lost their lives. Estimate what fraction of the soldiers lost their lives: _____

They also served in the navy and helped behind the battle lines. Harriet Tubman was called "the only American woman to lead troops on the field of battle." Find more information about these heroes.

J. Weston Walch, Publisher

Name _____ Date _____

ACTIVITY 21 ■ Benjamin Banneker's *Almanack*

Have you ever used an almanac? Several different almanacs are published every year. Each has about a thousand pages. There you can find information about all the countries of the world, people in sports, motion picture awards, and lots more. The numbers in some of the activities in this book come from almanacs.

In the early days of the United States most people did not own books, except for a family Bible and a yearly almanac. There were no calendars or daily weather forecasts. Farmers, shipmasters, and other people depended upon the almanac for this information. But how could anyone forecast the weather months ahead? The author of the almanac had to know astronomy and mathematics very well.

Such a person was Benjamin Banneker, a free African American born in 1730 in Maryland. Although he had very little schooling, he borrowed books and instruments to teach himself algebra, geometry, trigonometry, astronomy, and other sciences. His almanacs were widely used.

In 1791 Banneker sent the manuscript of his first *Almanack* to Thomas Jefferson, with a long letter. In this letter he criticized Jefferson for holding slaves. Jefferson was so impressed by the almanac that he sent it to the French Academy of Science.

This reproduction of the first page of the 1792 *Almanack* tells you what you might find in the book:

CONTAINING, the Motions of the Sun and Moon, the true Places and Aspects of the Planets, the Rising and Setting of the Sun, and the Rising, Setting and Southing, Place and Age of the Moon, etc.—The Lunations, Conjunctions, Eclipses, Judgment of the Weather, Festivals, and other remarkable Days . . .

and much more—tables of measures, recipes, essays and poems.

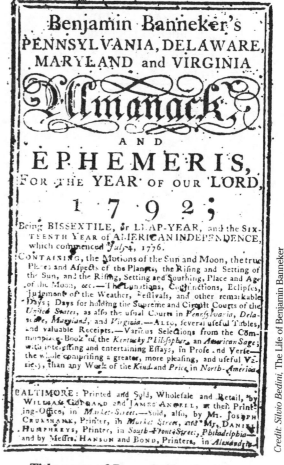

Title page of Banneker's almanac for 1792, published in Baltimore by Goddard & Angell

Credit: Silvio Bedini, The Life of Benjamin Banneker

J. Weston Walch, Publisher

Name _____   Date _____

ACTIVITY 21 ■ *(continued)*

Class Project

Form groups of three or four. Each group will design part of an almanac that would be of interest to the school.

Procedure

- List the topics that your group would like to write about. Then compare all the lists in the class to make sure that they are all different.

- For each topic, list the kind of information you will need and where you expect to find this information.

- Discuss and make notes on how you can bring mathematics into each topic (or most of the topics).

- Decide who will be responsible for each topic and each job (research, writing, art, etc.).

- Complete the almanac.

Think about this:

Banneker was well known as a scientist. When the new government decided to build the city of Washington as the capital of the United States, Banneker was chosen to a team of three men to survey and plan the site.

Look for more information about the scientist Benjamin Banneker. Discuss this information with the class.

Credit: Silvio Bedini, The Life of Benjamin Banneker

© 1987, 1993 Claudia Zaslavsky

J. Weston Walch, Publisher

Name _____   Date _____

ACTIVITY 22 ■ Change in Population of Four Cities

Some cities grew between 1970 and 1980, while others lost population. These are the population figures for four cities of different sizes, in 1970 and in 1980.

City	1970	1980
Anchorage, Alaska	48,081	173,017
Houston, Texas	1,233,535	1,594,066
New York, New York	7,895,563	7,071,030
Washington, D.C.	756,668	637,651

Complete the table below.

1. Round each population number to two significant figures (2 sf).

2. Find the approximate *amount* of increase or decrease in population from 1970 to 1980. Write a plus sign (+) in front of an increase, and a minus sign (–) in front of a decrease.

3. Find the *percent* of increase or decrease to the nearest whole number. Show your work below, as in the example. You may want to use a calculator.

City	Population (2 sf)		Increase or Decrease	
	1970	1980	Amount	Percent
Anchorage	48,000	170,000	+122,000	+254%
Houston				
New York				
Washington				

J. Weston Walch, Publisher

Name _____   Date _____

ACTIVITY 22 ■ *(continued)*

To find the percent (p) of change in population:

$$\frac{\text{Percent}}{100} = \frac{\text{Amount of change}}{\text{1970 population}}$$

Example: Anchorage

$$\frac{p}{100} = \frac{122,000}{48,000}$$

Reduce the fraction: $\dfrac{p}{100} = \dfrac{122}{48}$

$$p = (100 \times 122) \div 48 = 254\%$$

Think about this:

1. Arrange the four cities in order, from smallest to greatest, according to the change in population.

	Smallest	**Greatest**
Amount of change:		
Rate (percent) of change:		

2. Explain why the two lines in the table are different.

3. Look up the latest population of each city and compare it with the 1980 figure.

J. Weston Walch, Publisher

Name _____   Date _____

ACTIVITY 23 ▪ Growth of the Population of the United States

The population of the United States grew tremendously from 1820 to 1980. Did it increase at the same rate all through that period? Let's investigate.

U.S. POPULATION FROM 1820 TO 1980

Year	Population		Increase	
	Exact	Rounded (in millions)	Amount (in millions)	Rate (percent)
1820	9,638,453	10	—	—
1860	31,443,321	31	21	210%
1900	76,212,168			
1940	132,164,569			
1980	226,545,805			

Complete the table above.

1. Round the population figures to the nearest million. Notice that "population in millions" is at the top of the column.

2. Find the *amount* of increase, in millions, for each 40-year period.

3. Find the *rate* of increase, in percent, to the nearest whole number, for each 40-year period. Show your work on another sheet. Use the formula:

$$\frac{\text{Percent}}{100} = \frac{\text{Amount of increase}}{\text{Population in earlier year}}$$

Example: For the period 1820–1860,

$$\frac{p}{100} = \frac{21}{10}$$

$$p = (100 \times 21) \div 10 = 2100 \div 10 = 210\% \text{ increase}$$

Describe the *trend* (type of change) in the rate of increase from 1820 to 1980.

J. Weston Walch, Publisher

Name _____   Date _____

ACTIVITY 23 ■ *(continued)*

Think about this:

1. For the period 1820–1980, the amount of increase was about _____
   and the rate of increase was _____ . The population in 1980 was
   _____ times that in 1820. The 1820 population was _____ (fraction) of
   the 1980 population.

2. Estimate how many years it took for the population to double, starting in 1820
   _____ ; in 1860 _____ ; in 1900 _____ ; in 1940 _____ . Look up the latest population figure _____ .

J. Weston Walch, Publisher

Name _____   Date _____

ACTIVITY 24 ■ Spending Our Money: The Federal Budget

How big is a million? a billion? a trillion? Can you imagine spending a trillion dollars?

The budget of the United States government was about a trillion dollars for the year 1987. The government spent about $280 billion that year for military purposes. Let's see what that figure means.

Try to do some of the calculations mentally, using approximate numbers. Show necessary work in the space below.

1. Write $280 billion as a numeral: _____

2. If this sum were divided equally among all the 240 million people in the U.S., how much would each person pay?

   _____

3. On the average, about how much money is spent for military purposes:

   every week _____ ;   every day _____ ;

   every hour _____ ;   every minute _____ ?

4. The government spends more money than it takes in, and it must borrow money. In 1990 the national debt, the amount that the government owes, was over $3 trillion. Write this number as a numeral: _____ .

   If this sum were divided equally among all the people of the United States,

   each person would owe: _____ .

5. Find recent figures for the national debt and the federal budget. How was the money spent? (You might use an almanac.)

Think about this:

The national debt was over $3 trillion in 1990. If three trillion one-dollar bills were laid end to end, approximately how many times would they go around the equator, a distance of about 25,000 miles? A dollar bill is about 6 inches long. One mile equals 5,280 feet. Use approximate numbers, and show all your work on another sheet.

J. Weston Walch, Publisher

CHAPTER 3

Geometry and Measurement

Activities 25–36

Generally we don't think about the things around us in terms of geometry and measurement. Of course, every physical object has shape, size, and relationships to other objects. This chapter should enhance students' awareness of these properties.

The topics in this chapter are:

Activities 25, 26, 29, 30: Applications in several cultures of measurement and similarity in one, two, and three dimensions.

Activities 27 & 28: Geometry and measurement of the Great Pyramid and the Parthenon.

Activities 31–36: Symmetrical patterns in the art of the Hopi and Diné (Native American), Islamic, and other cultures.

REQUIRED MATERIALS

Activities 25, 26, 29: Grid paper.

Activity 27: Stiff paper, calculator.

Activity 28: Calculator.

Activities 31 & 32: Colored markers or crayons, computer (optional).

Activities 34 & 35: Compass, straightedge (ruler), art materials, pattern blocks (optional).

Activity 36: Isometric grid paper, straightedge (ruler), art materials, pattern blocks (optional).

Name _____   Date _____

ACTIVITY 25 ■ The Largest Garden Plot

Mary Jo and Wilbur plan to make a garden in the shape of a rectangle. They want to enclose the garden with 24 meters of wire fencing. Help them to find the dimensions of the biggest rectangle, the one with the most space for planting.

Call the longer side of the rectangle the *length*. Call the shorter side the *width*. The perimeter is 24 m (meters).

The smallest possible length is _____ m.

The greatest possible length is _____ m.

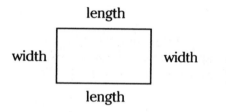

Guess the length of the largest possible rectangle: _____ m.

On a sheet of grid paper sketch rectangles A, B, C, D, and E. Use the scale: 1 unit = 1 m. Find the area of each rectangle by counting the small squares within the perimeter. Each small square represents one square meter (1 m²). Complete the table.

Rectangle	Length	Width	Area
A	6 m	6 m	36 m²
B	7 m		
C	8 m		
D	10 m		
E	11½ m		

J. Weston Walch, Publisher

Name _____   Date _____

ACTIVITY 25 ■ *(continued)*

The largest rectangle has

Area: _____ m²; length: _____ m; width: _____ m.

This type of rectangle is called a _____ .

The formula for the area of a rectangle is: Area = _____

Use this formula to check the areas in the table:

A: _____

B: _____

C: _____

D: _____

E: _____

Think about this:

In many societies around the world people build their own homes. They have no store-bought aids, like rulers or measuring tapes, to help them.

1. Name several societies in which people usually construct their own homes.

2. In some of these societies people live in rectangular houses. How can they be sure that the base is a rectangle? Remember—no commercial aids!

J. Weston Walch, Publisher

Name _____   Date _____

ACTIVITY 26 ■ The Shape of a House

Pretend that you are living in a society where people build their own homes, perhaps with the help of their relatives and neighbors. Since you must gather the materials yourself, you would like to construct a house that has the largest floor space for a given amount of materials for the walls. In mathematical language, you want to discover the shape that has the largest area for a given perimeter.

If you had a choice of a circle, an oval, and a square, which shape do you think has the largest area for a given perimeter? _____

Test several possible shapes for the floor by drawing the floor plans on graph paper and counting the small squares.

Choose a perimeter—32 units, for example. Tear off a strip of graph paper at least 32 units long, and mark the 32-unit length. Or you can use a string with a knot or mark at the 32-unit point.

1. Lay the paper strip or the string on the graph paper to form each figure in turn—a circle, an oval, and a square. Sketch the figure. Be sure that the perimeter is 32 units each time. (It helps to work with a classmate.)

Shape	Perimeter (units)	Area (square units)
Circle	32	
Oval	32	
Square	32	

J. Weston Walch, Publisher

Name _____   Date _____

ACTIVITY 26 ■ *(continued)*

2. Find the area of each shape by counting the small squares within the perimeter. Write the results in the table on the previous page.

   Conclusion: The _____ has the greatest area.

   Does this conclusion agree with your guess? _____

3. You may have had some difficulties in carrying out this project. How did you work them out?

   (a) How did you draw the circle?

   (b) How did you count the *fractions* of small squares?

   (c) Do you know a shortcut to avoid counting *all* the small squares? Describe it.

Think about this:

Name some societies in which people construct houses with circular floors. Describe the shapes of the houses, and sketch them. Perhaps you can build a model of such a house.

J. Weston Walch, Publisher

Name _____ Date _____

ACTIVITY 27 ■ The Wonderful Pyramids of Egypt

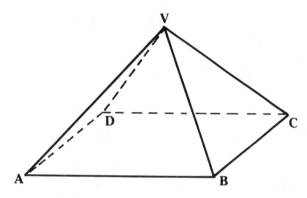

Considered one of the "Seven Wonders of the World" in ancient times, the Great Pyramid was built for Khufu, a pharaoh (king) of Egypt about 4,600 years ago. It is the largest of the many pyramids still standing in this part of Africa. People today wonder how the Egyptians carried out such tremendous construction projects without modern machinery.

The Great Pyramid has a square base measuring 756 feet along an edge. Each sloping side, called a *face* of the pyramid, is an isosceles triangle. The four triangles meet at a point called the *vertex*. The height is 481 feet (over 40 stories of a modern building), measured along an imaginary line from the vertex to the center of the base and perpendicular to the base. About 2.3 million stone blocks, weighing a total of 6 million tons, had to be cut and moved into place. The accuracy of measurement is mind-boggling.

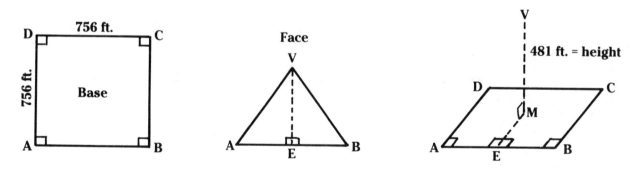

The organization of a labor force for such a gigantic task is impressive. It is estimated that it took 100,000 workers about 30 years, working during the three months of the year when the Nile River flooded the plains and farming was not possible. Imagine how much arithmetic and geometry went into the construction of just one pyramid!

1. Find the average weight of a stone block.

J. Weston Walch, Publisher

Name _____   Date _____

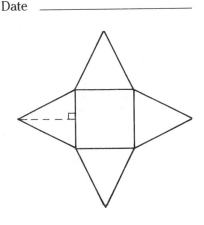

ACTIVITY 27 ■ *(continued)*

2. Construct a model of a pyramid out of stiff paper. First draw a square. Then construct four isosceles triangles, of equal height, one on each side of the square, as in the diagram. Copy the dotted line, the height of the isosceles triangle. This figure is called a *net*. Cut out the net, and fold it so that the dotted line is on the outside and the tips of the triangles meet at the vertex of the pyramid. Tape them together.

3. It is said that the area of one triangular face of the Great Pyramid is equal to the square of the height of the pyramid. Check this out. Do you have enough information to find the area of the triangle? You will need to find the height of the isosceles triangle, the dotted line on your model. [Hint: Use the right triangle relationship: $c^2 = a^2 + b^2$] Use a calculator for your computations, or round the numbers to make the work easier.

Think about this:

1. Some time before the construction of Khufu's pyramid, Imhotep, a great Egyptian scientist, designed the first stone pyramid. It is called the Step Pyramid because it consists of a set of stones laid one on top of the other, each square smaller than the one below it.

   Research and write a description of pyramid construction in ancient Egypt. Why were pyramids built? What is known about the methods of construction? How do you think the difficulties were solved?

2. Ancient Mexico was also the site of pyramid building. Not far from Mexico City are the Pyramid of the Sun and the Pyramid of the Moon, constructed 2,000 years ago. Other pyramids are scattered about Mexico and Guatemala. Find out more about these pyramids and write about them.

J. Weston Walch, Publisher

Name _____ Date _____

ACTIVITY 28 ■ The Golden Ratio

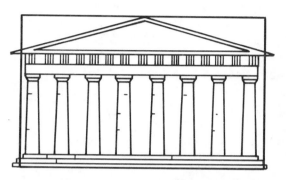

One of the most beautiful buildings of ancient times was the Parthenon, built in Greece almost 2,500 years ago. Many centuries earlier, the Egyptians and Mesopotamians had erected tremendous columned temples to their gods. You may see this style of architecture with columns in many public buildings, like the Capitol in Washington, D.C.

The diagram shows a sketch of the Parthenon (before it began to crumble) inside a rectangle. The ratio of the longer side to the shorter side of the rectangle is approximately 1.6 to 1. Another way to say this is that the longer side measures about 1.6 times the shorter side. A rectangle with these dimensions, called a *Golden Rectangle*, is said to be one of the most pleasing of geometric shapes. The ratio is called the *Golden Ratio*.

1. Measure the sides of the rectangle enclosing the Parthenon. How many centimeters is the longer side? the shorter side? Divide the larger number by the smaller and carry out the answer to one decimal place.

   Longer side _____ cm   Shorter side _____ cm   Ratio _____

   Is the answer close to 1.6, the Golden Ratio? What range of numbers should be considered "close to"? Would the numbers between 1.5 and 1.7 be close

   to 1.6? _____

2. Calculate the length of the longer side of a Golden Rectangle for each of the following shorter sides (try to do it mentally). Draw rectangle A in the space below.

   A: 4 cm   _____

   B: 15 cm   _____

   C: 3.5 m   _____

   D: 12½ ft   _____

3. Calculate the length of the shorter side of a Golden Rectangle for each of the following longer sides. (Draw rectangle E in the space below.)

   E: 3.2 cm   _____

   F: 40 in   _____

   G: $9 \frac{3}{5}$ ft   _____

                    J. Weston Walch, Publisher

Name _____   Date _____

ACTIVITY 28 ■ *(continued)*

4. A certain set of whole numbers is called a Fibonacci sequence. Here are the first few numbers in the set. Figure out the pattern; then write the next four numbers in the set.

    1, 1, 2, 3, 5, 8, 13, 21, _____ , _____ , _____ , _____ , · · ·

    Here is an interesting fact for you to discover. Find the ratio of each number, starting with 8, to the number before it, to two decimal places. Fill in the missing numbers below. You may use a calculator.

    (a) The ratio of 8 to 5 is _____ .

    (b) 13/8 = _____

    (c) 21/13 = _____

    (d)

    (e)

    (f)

    (g)

    Write the interesting fact: _____

    Fibonacci's father was an Italian merchant. The family lived for a long time in northern Africa. There Leonardo learned the advanced mathematics of Egypt, Syria, and nearby countries, written in the Arabic language. In the year 1202, when he was about 32 years old, Fibonacci published a mathematics book that soon became famous. This book helped to bring Indo-Arabic numerals to Europe.

Think about this:

In Activity 27 you learned about the Great Pyramid in Egypt. The square base measures 756 ft. along the edge. The height is 481 ft. Each sloping face is an isosceles triangle ($\triangle ABV$). In Activity 27 you found the altitude $\overline{EV}$. Now find the ratio of $\overline{EV}$ to $\overline{AE}$ to two decimal places. What do you discover?

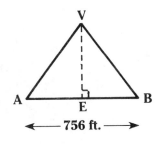

J. Weston Walch, Publisher

Name _____ Date _____

ACTIVITY 29 ▪ Stretching and Shrinking a Design

Dutch and English settlers brought the art of quiltmaking to America. The quilting party, called a "quilting bee," was a favorite social activity among women of both European and African backgrounds. Some of the most beautiful of these quilts have been preserved in museums.

Some quilts were constructed of small squares, each embroidered in a different design. The basket pattern below appears on a quilt that is now in the Metropolitan Museum of Art in New York.

The quiltmaker decides to enlarge the design to fit the larger square. Copy the pattern on the grid of the large square.

The quiltmaker has to estimate the quantity of material and embroidery thread that she will need. As a first step, compare the two squares.

1. The length of the side of the large square is _____ times that of the small square.

2. The small square has a quarter-inch grid. The area of the basket (without the handle) is _____ sq. in., consisting of _____ sq. in. of dark sections and _____ sq. in. of light sections.

3. The large square has a half-inch grid. The area of the basket (without the handle) is _____ sq. in., consisting of _____ sq. in. of dark sections and _____ sq. in. of light sections.

4. The large basket requires _____ times as much material as the small basket.

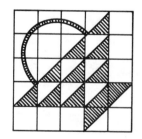

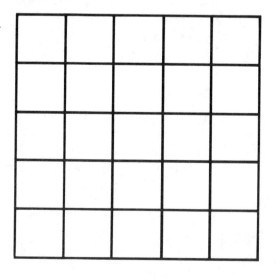

J. Weston Walch, Publisher

Name _____   Date _____

ACTIVITY 29 ■ *(continued)*

Think about this:

In former times both men and women in eastern Europe wore shirts and other garments trimmed with colorful bands of embroidery. On each band a complex geometric pattern was repeated over and over again.

On a separate sheet of grid paper, draw a geometric motif that can be repeated to make a neckband for a man's shirt.

On the same sheet draw this motif again to fit the neckband of a small boy's shirt. Each dimension should be half that of the original design.

J. Weston Walch, Publisher

Name _____   Date _____

ACTIVITY 30 ■ Similar Shapes in Three Dimensions

The Chagga people live on the slopes of Mount Kilimanjaro in Tanzania, Africa. Traditionally they built their thatched houses in the shape of a bee-hive. The Kibo Art Gallery, on the mountain slope, includes a thatched building *similar* in shape to an ordinary Chagga house, but three times as tall and three times as wide. If both buildings have walls of the same thickness, estimate how many times as much thatch the art gallery building requires:

_____ times as much thatch.

We can experiment with two parallelepipeds (boxes) that are similar in shape. The dimensions of the smaller box are 2 in. × 4 in. × 3 in. The larger box has twice the dimensions of the smaller. Draw and label the large box.

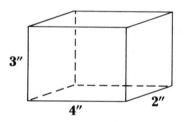

1. *Surface area* (SA) of a box is the sum of the areas of all six sides. Compare the SAs of the two boxes.

	Top or bottom	**Front or back**	**Side**	**Total surface area**
Small box	2 × 4 = 8 sq. in.	3 × 4 = 12 sq. in.	2 × 3 = 6 sq. in.	2(8 + 12 + 6) = 52 sq. in.
Large box				

Ratio: SA of the large box is _____ times the SA of the small box.

J. Weston Walch, Publisher

Name _____   Date _____

ACTIVITY 30 ■ *(continued)*

2. Compare the *volumes* (V) of the two boxes, measured in cubic inches. Pretend that you are filling the boxes with 1-inch cubes. The volume of each cube is 1 cubic inch (cu. in.).

   Small box: _____ cubes fill one layer, and _____ layers fill the box.

   The box holds _____ 1-inch cubes. Volume = _____ cu. in.

   Large box: _____ cubes fill one layer, and _____ layers fill the box.

   The box holds _____ 1-inch cubes. Volume = _____ cu. in.

   Ratio: The volume of the large box is _____ times the volume of the small box.

3. Show your work to compare a 3-inch cube with a 1-inch cube.

	Large cube	**Small cube**	**Ratio: large to small**
Length of side	3 in.	1 in.	3 to 1
Surface area			
Volume			

Think about this:

1. Look at your estimate for the amount of thatch for the Kibo Art Gallery. Do you agree with it? Explain.

2. Two cylinders (cans) have similar shapes. One has four times the dimensions of the other. Show how you can compare their surface areas and volumes without the use of formulas. What conclusions do you expect? Use another sheet, if necessary.

J. Weston Walch, Publisher

Name _____   Date _____

ACTIVITY 31 ■ Border Patterns

The Diné (also known as Navajo) people of the southwestern United States often use zigzag designs in their beautiful handwoven rugs.

Use this zigzag design to finish the borders below. For each border, continue the pattern that has been started. Then color the borders.

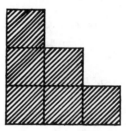

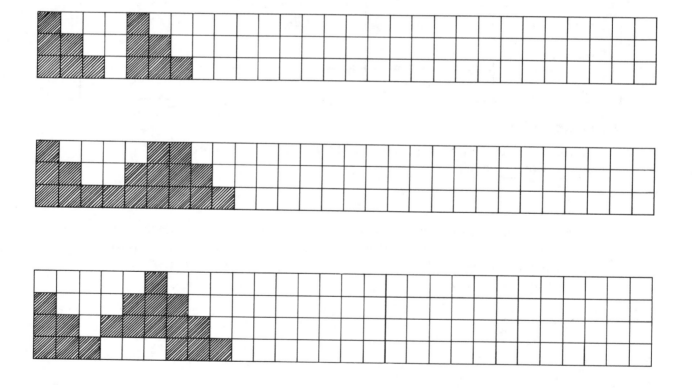

J. Weston Walch, Publisher

Name _____   Date _____

ACTIVITY 31 ■ *(continued)*

Think about this:

1. Make up a design, and repeat it any way you like in this border. Then color the border.

2. Can you do computer graphics? If you can, you may be able to write a program that can do the graphics for a repeated pattern. Try it.

J. Weston Walch, Publisher

Name _____ Date _____

ACTIVITY 32 ▪ Symmetry in Diné Art

Nearly a thousand years the Diné (Dee-nay) people migrated from the north-western region of North America to the southwest of the land now called the United States. The Spanish conquerors of the Southwest called them the "Navajo" (Nah-vah-ho). In the sixteenth century, Spanish settlers brought sheep to the region, and the Diné became sheepherders.

From the neighboring Pueblo Indians, Diné women learned to weave on looms. Soon they were making beautiful woolen blankets, rugs, and clothing. These weavers did not use written patterns or instructions, yet they were able to weave complicated symmetrical designs. Some of their blankets and rugs, often called the "first American tapestries," are now in museums for everyone to admire.

This is a part of a Diné blanket, shown as it hung on a wall. Imagine that you can fold the blanket so that one half of the design matches the other half. Where is the *fold line*? Actually there are two fold lines, one vertical and the other horizontal, as shown by the dashed lines on the rectangle below the blanket. Now turn your paper so that the writing is upside down. Yet the design on the blanket appears to be the same as in the right-side-up position. We say the design has *rotational* (also called *turn*) symmetry. It looks the same in two different positions as it is turned.

Look at the design in one quarter of the grid on the next page. The rectangle has two lines of symmetry, one vertical and the other horizontal. Think of each symmetry line as a mirror (you may want to use a mirror). Copy the mirror image of the design in each of the three blank quarters of the rectangle. The design should have rotational symmetry, also. Then fill in the uncolored sections in pleasing earth colors.

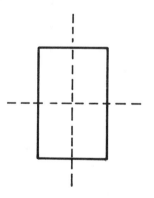

J. Weston Walch, Publisher

Name _____ Date _____

ACTIVITY 32 ■ *(continued)*

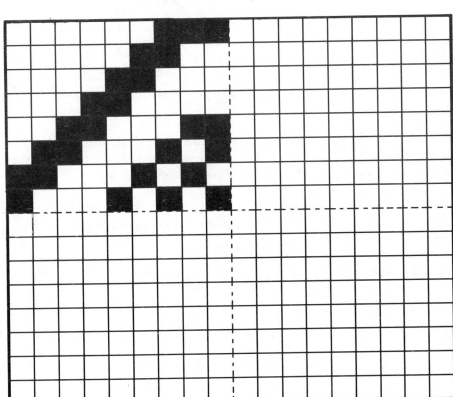

Think about this:

1. Design half of a Diné-type rug with a zigzag border (see Activity 31), so that the pattern has line symmetry. You may want to use a sheet of grid paper. Exchange your design with a classmate and complete his or her rug so that it has rotational symmetry.

2. Can you do computer graphics? Try to write a program that will repeat a design for a rug.

J. Weston Walch, Publisher

Name _____   Date _____

ACTIVITY 33 ■ The Symmetry of Symbols

Each of the designs below has some meaning. These designs are called *symbols*. By wearing or displaying such a symbol, a person expresses a thought or a feeling.

Look at each symbol. Does the design have symmetry? Here are the two types of symmetry to look for:

1. *Line symmetry.* Imagine that you try to fold each design in half so that one half fits exactly over the other half. The design may have more than one such *fold line*, or none at all. Draw all the possible fold lines.

2. *Turn symmetry.* Does the pattern look the same when you turn this sheet to a different position? In how many positions does the design look the same? Be sure to count the original position.

Fill in the chart on the next page with your answers.

(a) Love

(b) Peace

(c) Chinese Yin-Yang: "Unity of opposites"

(d) Star

(e) Ghana: "Unity is strength"

(f) Canada: Maple leaf

(g) Ankh—"Life": Ancient Egypt

J. Weston Walch, Publisher

Name _____   Date _____

ACTIVITY 33 ■ *(continued)*

Symbol	(a)	(b)	(c)	(d)	(e)	(f)	(g)
Number of fold lines	1						
Number of turn positions	1						

Think about this:

Draw several symbols that have symmetry. You may copy a logo for a product, a symbol on a flag, or make up your own. Describe the symmetry of each symbol. Work on another sheet.

J. Weston Walch, Publisher

Name _____   Date _____

ACTIVITY 34 ■ The Symmetry of Hopi Baskets

Fifteen hundred years ago the Anasazi, a Native American tribe living in the Southwest, were weaving flat coiled baskets. Today their descendants, the Hopi of northern Arizona, continue the tradition. Here are several patterns that Hopi women incorporate in their fine woven baskets.

Examine each basket, and write the answers to questions 1 and 2 in the table on the next page. Basket A is an example.

1. *Line, or bilateral, symmetry.* Can you draw a diameter that will divide the basket into two matching parts, so that one half is a mirror image of the other? How many such diameters can be drawn? This number is the *order of bilateral symmetry.*

2. *Turn, or rotational, symmetry.* Place your fingertip or pencil point on the center of the basket. Turn the page slowly, until the pattern looks the same as when you started. In how many different positions does the design appear to be the same, counting the starting position? This number is the *order of rotational symmetry.*

(a)
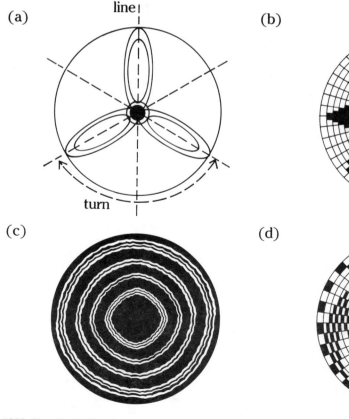

(b)
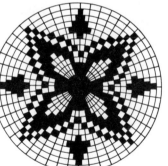

(c)
(d)

J. Weston Walch, Publisher

Name _____   Date _____

ACTIVITY 34 ■ *(continued)*

Order of symmetry	(a)	(b)	(c)	(d)
Bilateral	3			
Rotational	3			

In the circle draw a pattern for a Hopi-style basket that has turn symmetry of order two, but no lines of symmetry.

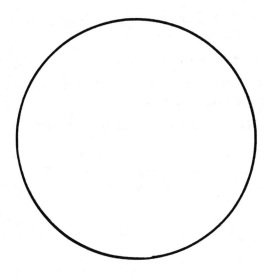

Think about this:

Draw a design for a Hopi-style basket that has both line (bilateral) and turn (rotational) symmetry of order six. You may want to use a compass to make the pattern.

J. Weston Walch, Publisher

Name _____ Date _____

ACTIVITY 35 ■ Islamic Art: Design

Islam is a religion with a very rich geometric art. From India to Spain, the artists of Islam have been creating and repeating these geometric patterns for over a thousand years. Their beautiful designs decorate floors and ceilings, walls and doors, rugs and bowls, and the pages of books. Yet all these patterns are formed with just a compass and a straightedge.

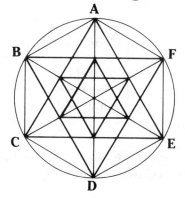

1. Look at this construction. Can you copy it on another sheet? You will need a compass and a straightedge (ruler).

   • Draw a circle having a radius of 5 cm.

   • With the compass set at the same radius, use the compass to mark off along the circle the points A, B, C, D, E, and F.

   • Connect all six points with straight lines in as many ways as possible.

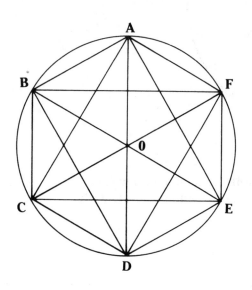

2. The diagram at left shows your construction at this stage. The center of the circle is marked O.

   (a) The figure connecting points A, B, C, D, E, F, and A in that order is called

   a _____ .
   Each edge of this shape measures

   _____ cm.

   (b) On the back of this sheet, list everything you know about triangles ACE and BDF.

   (c) Describe the shape formed by overlapping triangles ACE and BDF:

   _____

3. Complete the construction and color it.

Think about this:

Draw an original design using only a compass and straightedge, and color it.

J. Weston Walch, Publisher

Name _____   Date _____

ACTIVITY 36 ■ Islamic Art: Tessellations

With the circle as the basis, Islamic artists created repeated patterns that covered whole surfaces of walls and floors. These patterns are called *tessellations*. Here is an example. It is a copy of the tiled wall in a painting in the *Shāh-nāmeh*, the *Book of Kings* of Persia (now Iran).

Adapted from the Shāh-nāmeh,
The Book of Kings

You have probably seen tiled floors in bathrooms and kitchens. Of course, they are not as beautiful as the wall in the painting. A tiled panel like this might be found in a mosque or a palace.

1. Name the geometric shapes that you find in this pattern. Look for combinations

    that form other shapes. _____

    _____

It is easy to draw a repeated pattern of geometric shapes on grid paper. Ordinary graph paper is already a repeated pattern of squares. Isometric (meaning "having the same measure") grid paper is a repeated pattern of dots that form equilateral triangles. In each triangle the three sides are equal and each angle measures 60°. You can combine two or more small triangles to make a rhombus (diamond), a trapezoid, or a hexagon.

2. On isometric grid paper repeat each shape several times so that it covers a portion of the paper:

    (a) rhombus   (b) trapezoid   (c) hexagon

J. Weston Walch, Publisher

Name _____   Date _____

ACTIVITY 36 ▪ *(continued)*

Describe the measure of the angles of each of the three shapes: _____

_____

Islamic artists usually start by drawing one shape. Then they spread outward in all directions from that shape. Look at the copy of the tiled panel. Find a hexagon near the center. See how the pattern grows around it.

3. Here are some hints to help you draw a six-pointed star tessellation on isometric paper.

   Step 1. Outline a hexagon in the center of the area you plan to use. Color or shade it, or draw a decoration inside it. That way you will know your starting place.

   Step 2. Outline six hexagons around the first hexagon so that each hexagon shares one point with the first hexagon. This is the same idea as placing six pennies around a penny in the center so that their edges touch (try that first).

   Step 3. Shade or color the six hexagons. The unshaded triangles between the hexagons form the points of the stars. The stars share their points.

   Step 4. Continue the pattern.

Think about this:

1. You and your classmates might make your own tile panel of construction paper or gift wrapping paper. Cut out many hexagons, all the same size. Decorate them as you like. Then attach the shapes to a large sheet of oaktag, according to the directions in exercise 3.

2. Use pattern blocks to make a repeated pattern. Trace the pattern on paper and color it.

J. Weston Walch, Publisher

CHAPTER 4

Probability, Statistics, and Graphs

Activities 37–47

We often think of numbers in terms of getting the right answer. But in life we have to deal with a great degree of uncertainty. In this chapter students will perform experiments to learn about probability, the mathematics of uncertainty. They will also handle real-world problems involving charts, tables, and graphs.

The topics in this chapter are:

Activities 37–39: Outcomes and probabilities relating to tossing fair coins and asymmetrical cowrie (macaroni) shells. Ways of "predicting the future" in various societies of Asia and Africa.

Activities 40–42: Statistics and graphs about eating and smoking.

Activities 43–45: Statistics and graphs about infant mortality rates and rates of population growth.

Activities 46 & 47: Statistics and graphs about the federal budget.

PREPARATION AND REQUIRED MATERIALS

Activity 37: Coins.

Activity 38: Macaroni shells or thumb tacks.

Activity 40: Students collect labels on food packages.

Activities 40 & 41: Ask students to do the writing assignment (Exercise 1) before you distribute the activity sheets.

Activity 42: Before students carry out the activity, contact an antismoking organization for ideas and materials. See "Think About This" for the address of Stop Teenage Addiction to Tobacco (STAT).

Activity 43: Grid paper, rulers, calculators.

Activity 44: Almanac or other reference book, calculators (optional).

Activity 45: Grid paper, rulers, almanac.

Activity 46: Rulers, calculators (optional).

Activity 47: Calculators, compass, rulers, protractors.

Name _____   Date _____

ACTIVITY 37 ▪ What Are the Outcomes? (Part 1): Toss a Coin or Two

People have always wanted to know what would happen in the future. Diviners and fortune tellers have claimed to foresee the future by reading the stars or examining the inner organs of a chicken.

A simpler way is to toss a coin. Only two outcomes are possible, heads or tails. If the coin is fair (balanced), it is equally likely to land heads up or tails up.

When you toss a coin many times, you *expect* it to come up heads one-half the time. The *expected* probability of heads is:

$$\text{Probability (heads)} = P(H) = \frac{1}{2} = 0.5$$

In practice, though, the number of heads may be more or less than half the total number of tosses.

Experiment 1. Toss a coin ten times, and tally the number of heads and the number of tails. [Tally: 卌 = 5.] Repeat for ten more tosses, and continue until you have tossed the coin fifty times. After each set of ten tosses, write the success fraction for heads, in both common fraction and decimal fraction form.

$$\text{Success fraction (SF)} = \frac{\text{Total number of heads}}{\text{Total number of tosses}}$$

Write the difference between each success fraction and 0.5, the *expected* probability of a head.

	10	20	30	40	50
Heads					
Tails					
SF	$\frac{}{10} =$	$\frac{}{20} =$	$\frac{}{30} =$		
Difference					

J. Weston Walch, Publisher

Name _____   Date _____

ACTIVITY 37 ■ *(continued)*

Experiment 2. Toss two coins 12 times—for example, a penny and a nickel. Write the outcome for each toss: H or T.

Toss	1	2	3	4	5	6	7	8	9	10	11	12
Penny												
Nickel												

Summarize the results: H, H _____ times;   T, T _____ times;

H, T _____ times;   T, H _____ times.

Think about this:

1. Analyze the results of Experiment 1.

2. Write the expected probability for each result when two fair coins are tossed:

    P (2 heads) = _____   P (1 head) = _____   P (0 heads) = _____

    Do these probabilities agree with your results in Experiment 2?

3. Investigate a game of chance. One example is the Dreidel game played on the Jewish holiday Hanukkah, the Festival of Lights, which occurs in December. A dreidel is a four-sided top.

Drawn by Sam Zaslavsky

4. Do you think it is possible to know what will happen in the future? Discuss this question. Write up your opinions and reasons on a separate piece of paper.

                    J. Weston Walch, Publisher

Name _____   Date _____

ACTIVITY 38 ■ What Are the Outcomes? (Part 2): Toss a Cowrie Shell

People often make a "yes or no" decision by tossing a coin. A fair coin has *symmetry*; it is just as likely to show a head as a tail.

In the past, and even in recent times, some societies in Africa and Asia used cowrie shells as money. Cowrie shells were also used in fortune-telling and gambling games. A cowrie shell does *not* have symmetry.

Instead of cowrie shells, you may use macaroni shells or thumbtacks in the following experiments.

Experiment 1. Toss a shell or thumbtack 10 times, and tally the number of times it lands with the opening (or point) up or down. Repeat for 10 more tosses, and continue until you have tossed the shell (or tack) 50 times.

After each set of 10 tosses, write the success fraction (SF) for "opening up" (or "point up"), in both common fraction and decimal form.

$$\text{Success fraction (SF)} = \frac{\text{Total number up}}{\text{Total number of tosses}}$$

	10	20	30	40	50
Up					
Down					
SF (up)	$\overline{10}$ =	$\overline{20}$ =	$\overline{30}$ =		

Experiment 2.

Materials: Two macaroni shells, one marked, the other unmarked.

Procedure: Toss the two shells 20 times. Record the outcomes on the next page. Write U for "opening up," and D for "opening down."

J. Weston Walch, Publisher

Name _____   Date _____

ACTIVITY 38 ■ *(continued)*

Toss	1	2	3	4	5	6	7	8	9	10	11	12	13	14	15	16	17	18	19	20
Marked																				
Unmarked																				

Summarize the results: U, U _____ times;   D, D _____ times;

U, D _____ times;   D, U _____ times.

Think about this:

1. Examine the results in Experiment 2. Are they what you expect? Why or why not? Write your answer on the back of this sheet.

2. For more than 2,000 years the *I Ching*, or *Book of Changes*, has been used in China, Korea, and Japan to foretell the future. The system is based on arrangements of two types of lines, solid and broken, in groups of three. Here are three such groups:

Flag of South Korea

   (a) Draw all the remaining groups of lines. The total number is _____ .

   (b) How can you figure out the total number of groups without having to draw them?

   (c) *I Ching* has a set of wise sayings for each arrangement of six lines. At right is one arrangement.

   The person who consults *I Ching* has to figure out how these wise words apply to his or her problem. People really have to make their own decisions about their future.

J. Weston Walch, Publisher

Name _____   Date _____

ACTIVITY 39 ■ What Are the Outcomes? (Part 3): Toss More Coins and Shells

A popular game in eastern Nigeria is called "Pitch and Toss," or *Igba-ita* in the Igbo language. Formerly it was played with cowrie shells. Now it is played with coins, and the name has been changed to *Igba-ego* (*ego* means "money"). Here is a simple version.

Each player has a heap of cowrie shells. One player, the challenger, picks up four shells, while the others each drop one or two shells on a pile in the center. The challenger tosses his or her four shells and notes how they land. If the openings are all up, all down, or two up and two down, he or she wins all the shells in the center. Otherwise the challenger adds the four shells to the pile in the center.

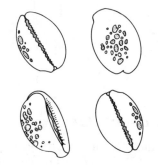

Suppose you were playing the game with coins instead of shells. A coin is equally likely to land heads up or tails up. Write out all the possible outcomes when four different coins are tossed. Here are three:

H   H   H   H

H   H   H   T

H   H   T   H

1. The total number of different outcomes is _____ .

2. Write each probability (P) as a fraction.

$$P = \frac{\text{Expected number of heads}}{\text{Total number of outcomes}}$$

P (4 H) = _____   P (2 H) = _____   P (0 H) = _____

P (3 H) = _____   P (1 H) = _____

J. Weston Walch, Publisher

Name _____   Date _____

ACTIVITY 39 ■ *(continued)*

3. The sum of all the fractions in exercise 2 is:

    _____ + _____ + _____ + _____ + _____ = _____

4. The sum in exercise 3 should be 1. Why?

5. In the game of *Igba-ego*, find the sum of winning probabilities and the sum of the losing probabilities. Is the challenger more likely to win or to lose? Why?

Think about this:

1. Suppose you toss five coins. How many different combinations of heads and tails would you expect? Explain your answer.

2. How many different outcomes are possible when six coins are tossed? _____

3. The Yoruba people of western Nigeria have long practiced the *Ifa* system of foretelling the future. The diviner tosses a chain of eight half-shells and notes the position of each half-shell, whether it opens up or down. Find the total number of combinations. How did you get your answer?

    Each arrangement is associated with a set of wise sayings. A person decides how these sayings connect to his or her problem.

Ifa Chain

J. Weston Walch, Publisher

Name _____ Date _____

ACTIVITY 40 ▪ What Do You Eat?

1. (a) On another sheet make a list of the foods you ate the last time you had lunch. Next to each food write the quantity. For example:

Bread	2 slices
Cheese	2½ slices
Milk (whole)	8 ounces

   (b) Exchange your list with a classmate. Do you know how many calories and how much fat, sugar, and salt she or he ate?

People are becoming more health conscious. They are concerned about what's in their food. Many people think that they would be healthier if they cut down on their intake of fat, sugar, salt, and total calories.

Packaged foods must be labeled to show the ingredients. Here is some of the information on a box of dry cereal:

Nutrition Information per Serving	
Serving size	1 ounce
Calories	140
Protein	3 g
Carbohydrates	29 g (grams)
Fat	3 g
Sodium (salt)	330 mg (milligrams)

The package label gives the ingredients in a one-ounce serving of cereal. But adults usually eat portions that are larger than one ounce. Bread manufacturers consider a serving to be one slice. Do you think that one slice of bread is enough for a serving? How many slices go into a sandwich?

For the past few years, food manufacturers and packagers have been listing smaller and smaller serving sizes on their packages. That way they can make their products appear to have less of the ingredients that people worry about.

2. Consider that the usual serving of a dry cereal is 1½ ounces. Calculate the amount of each ingredient in a serving of the cereal described above. On the next page, make up a label to show the "Nutrition Information per Serving."

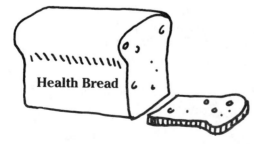

J. Weston Walch, Publisher

Name _____   Date _____

ACTIVITY 40 ■ *(continued)*

Nutrition Information per Serving

Here are the listings on the labels of two packages of sliced bread:

	HEALTH BREAD		**GREAT BREAD**	
	Label	**Usual**	**Label**	**Usual**
Serving size	1 slice		1 slice	
Weight of package	16 oz	—	24 oz	—
Number of slices	16		18	—
Weight per serving		2 oz		2 oz
Calories	60		70	
Carbohydrates	10 g		12 g	
Fat	1 g		1 g	
Sodium	120 mg		135 mg	

J. Weston Walch, Publisher

Name _____   Date _____

ACTIVITY 40 ■ *(continued)*

3. (a) Complete the table on the previous page. Assume that a person usually eats two ounces of bread at one serving. What amount of each ingredient would she or he eat?

    (b) Suppose that you want to limit your intake of calories, carbohydrates, fats, and salt. Which bread would you choose if you compare the quantities of ingredients:

    Listed on the labels? _____

    In the usual serving of two ounces? _____

    Write your reasons for the choice.

Think about this:

Work with your group. Examine the labels on different brands of a certain food: bread, dry cereals, cheese, etc. Note the serving sizes and quantities of the various ingredients listed on the packages. Make a table to compare the information for the different brands of one particular food.

Find out what people consider the usual serving size of that food. How can you do that? Compare your results with the information on the labels. Write a report on your research.

                    J. Weston Walch, Publisher

Name _____   Date _____

ACTIVITY 41 ▪ To Smoke or Not to Smoke (Part 1): Why Die Young?

You have probably dreamed about the kind of life you would like to have in the future. Picture your life 25 years from now—your career, your family, how you spend your free time.

Credit: Melissa Antonow, Grade Five, New York City

1. On another sheet write a paragraph describing your life in the future. Exchange your paragraph with another student. Is your vision similar to your classmate's?

Right now some of your classmates may be destroying their dreams of a healthy, happy future. The killer is tobacco. But tobacco is a slow, tormenting killer. It is not quick, like a gunshot or a car accident. Although the percentage of Americans who smoke is lower now than in the past, the number of deaths from smoking and smokefree tobacco (snuff) is higher. So says a 1991 report by the National Centers for Disease Control.

Does this sound like a contradiction? Dr. William L. Roper, director of the Centers, explains. "The problem is, we are now paying for what happened 20 or 30 years ago, when large numbers of people smoked in large amounts" [*New York Times* (2/1/91)]. About half of all smokers started their habit by the age of 13. Later, they found that they could not give up the habit.

Here are some figures from the 1991 report:

Deaths from smoking (in thousands)		
	1965	**1988**
Women	30	147
Men	158	287
TOTAL	188	424

Percentage who smoked each year		
	1965	**1988**
Women	32%	26%
Men	50%	31%

J. Weston Walch, Publisher

Name _____   Date _____

ACTIVITY 41 ■ *(continued)*

2. Use the two tables to supply the missing numbers.

   (a) How many people died of smoking in 1965? _____ ;

   in 1988? _____

   (b) For men, the 1988 deaths are about _____ times the 1965 deaths.

   For women, the 1988 deaths are about _____ times the 1965 figure.

   (c) The highest percentage of smokers was among _____ in the year

   _____.

   The lowest percentage of smokers was among _____ in the year

   _____.

   (d) Did women or men do better at not smoking from 1965 to 1988? Discuss this question with your group or class. Give reasons for your answers.

   The government report discusses smoking among various groups:
   - More young people than older people are smokers.
   - In 1988 blacks had a higher death rate from smoking than whites.
   - Women are slower than men to give up smoking.

   But there is hope. Dr. Roper said, "It is never too late to quit."

   The tobacco industry spends a large amount of money on advertising, a sum of $3.26 billion in 1988. In that year their profits were nearly $7 billion. But in the same year the cost to the nation was about $65 billion in medical costs and days lost from work due to cigarettes.

3. Calculate the average amount for each day in 1988 (nearest $1,000,000):

   (a) Spent on tobacco advertising _____

   (b) Profits of the tobacco industry _____

   (c) Cost of illness due to cigarettes _____

Think about this:

Work with several classmates to keep a record of the ads you see. You might find them on billboards, in stores, in magazines and newspapers, in movies. Although cigarette ads are banned from TV, they often appear on billboards in athletic stadiums during telecasts of games.

Decide how you will do the survey and how many days it will cover. Then write a newspaper article about your findings.

J. Weston Walch, Publisher

Name _____   Date _____

ACTIVITY 42 ■ To Smoke or Not to Smoke (Part 2): Who Pays?

Many people don't realize that tobacco is such a killer. That may be because tobacco is a legal drug. But the number of deaths tells the story.

1. Make a pie chart to compare deaths from smoking in 1988 with several other causes of death. Complete the table. You may want to use a calculator. You will need a compass and protractor to draw the graph.

Cause of death	Number	Percent	Degrees
Smoking	434,000	64%	
Alcohol	105,000		
Car accidents	49,000		
AIDS	31,000		
Suicide & homicide	53,000		
Drugs	6,000		
TOTAL	678,000	100%	360°

It is not only smokers and users of snuff who die of cancer, heart disease, respiratory and other diseases caused by tobacco. People may also suffer from other people's smoking, called "passive smoke" or "second-hand smoke." Government agencies believe that 53,000 people die every year of passive smoke, in the workplace or the home.

PACK OF LIES

HEALTHY ATHLETIC SAFE MATURE SEXY

Cigarettes

The Truth: *Smoking stains your teeth yellow, gives you camel breath, makes your clothes stink, and offends everyone around you.*

*Smoking also causes lung cancer, throat cancer, stroke, emphysema, heart disease, and fetal injury!

Credit: Caheim Drake, Grade Four, Bronx, New York

J. Weston Walch, Publisher

Name _____   Date _____

ACTIVITY 42 ■ *(continued)*

In June 1991 the National Center for Health Statistics found, according to the *New York Times* (6/19/91):

- In households with smokers, 4.1 percent of children were in poor health. In smokefree homes, 2.4 percent of children were in poor health. Of course, other factors may cause poor health.

- Two-thirds of children in low-income homes were exposed to smoke, as compared with 36 percent of children in higher-income homes.

- Children of nonsmokers had higher scores in tests of reasoning ability.

Many cities and states now have Clean Indoor Air Acts. These laws tell people where they may or may not smoke in public places. Many schools ban smoking altogether. But some smokers feel they should be able to smoke indoors under certain conditions. They have asked their representatives in government to sponsor a "Smokers' Bill of Rights." The tobacco industry supports such bills.

2. (a) Find out whether your town and state have Clean Indoor Air Acts, and what they say.

   (b) Work with your group from Activity 41. Pretend that you are a lobbying group, people who pressure legislators to pass certain laws. Decide whether you want a Clean Indoor Air Act or a Smokers' Bill of Rights. Prepare the arguments you will use when you appear before the State Legislature.

Think about this:

Students in schools around the country have decided to take action against smoking. They make posters that are exhibited in buses and trains. They try to talk to the managers of ball teams about advertising in the stadiums. They have marches and meetings, write letters, and sign petitions.

Discuss with your classmates whether your school should join in such actions against the use of tobacco. Write a plan. For more information, contact Stop Teenage Addiction to Tobacco (STAT), 121 Lyman Street, Suite 210, Springfield, MA 01103; (413) 732-7828.

J. Weston Walch, Publisher

Name _____   Date _____

ACTIVITY 43 ■ Infant Mortality: Why Do Babies Die?

The infant mortality rate tells how many babies die before their first birthday, for every 1,000 live births.

These are the infant mortality rates for 10 countries for the year 1988:

Australia 9   Mexico 46

Cuba 15   Poland 16

France. 8   Saudi Arabia. 70

Japan 5   South Africa 71

Kenya 71   United States 10

1. Which country had the highest rate of infant deaths?

   _____

   the lowest rate?

   _____

2. Which countries had a better record than the United States?

   _____

3. Compare infant mortality in the following countries with that of the United States. Use approximate numbers and mental arithmetic.

   Example: Poland—about __1½__ times U.S.

   Saudi Arabia: _____ ;

   South Africa: _____ ;

   Cuba: _____ ;

   Japan: _____ .

J. Weston Walch, Publisher

Name _____   Date _____

ACTIVITY 43 ■ *(continued)*

4. Calculate the infant mortality rate in the U.S. for the year 1990.

    Data: 4,179,000 live births; 38,100 infant deaths

    Set up a proportion to find the death rate per 1,000 live births, and solve it. How can you know that your answer is reasonable?

5. On graph paper draw a bar graph to compare infant mortality rates in the 10 countries in 1988. Check your answers to question 3 by measuring the lengths of the bars. Which answers would you change?

Think about this:

These are approximate figures for infant mortality in the U.S. in the year 1987:

	Mortality rate per 1,000 live births	Number of deaths	Number of live births
Total U.S.	10	38,000	
White infants	9	26,000	
Black infants	18	11,000	
Other infants	15	1,000	

Use a calculator to find the approximate number of live births for each group to the nearest 100,000. Show all work below and on the back of this sheet. How do you know that your answers are reasonable?

How do you account for the higher death rate of black infants? Research this question and discuss it. Write up your conclusions.

J. Weston Walch, Publisher

Name _____   Date _____

ACTIVITY 44 ■ Population of California

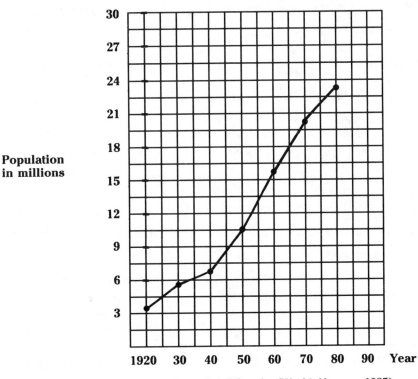

**Population
in millions**

Population of California (*World Almanac* 1985)

This graph shows the growth in the population of California from 1920 to 1980. Every 10 years, in the years ending in zero, the population of the United States is counted in the census. The dots on the graph give the census figures for those years. The dots are connected by straight lines.

In 1980 California was the most populous state in the country. Answer the questions about the population by reading the graph.

Year	1920	1930	1940	1950	1960	1970	1980
Population (in millions)	3						

J. Weston Walch, Publisher

Name _____   Date _____

ACTIVITY 44 ■ *(continued)*

1. Complete the table on the previous page. Write the approximate population, to the nearest million.

2. Estimate the population in 1975: _____ ; in 1952 _____ .

3. The population in 1980 was about _____ times that of 1920, and about _____ times that of 1950.

4. Which 10-year period shows the greatest increase in population? _____ . The increase was about _____ million.

5. In the decade 1970–1980, the *amount* of increase was _____ million. The *percent* of increase was _____ %, based on the 1970 population. Use the following proportion:

$$\frac{\text{Amount of increase}}{\text{1970 population}} = \frac{\text{Percent increase}}{100}$$

6. In the decade 1960–1970, the *amount* of increase was _____ and the *percent* was _____ .

7. (a) Use the graph on the previous page to predict the population in 1990: _____ .

   (b) Look up the 1990 population in a reference book: _____ .

   Was your prediction correct? _____ .

   (c) Extend the graph to 1990.

   (d) In the decade 1980–1990, the amount of increase was _____ and the percent of increase was _____ .

Think about this:

Why did the population of California grow so rapidly?

J. Weston Walch, Publisher

Name _____ Date _____

ACTIVITY 45 ■ Population of New York State

Until about 1965, when California pulled ahead, New York was the most populous state in the country.

The table gives the census figures for the population of New York State from 1920 to 1990, rounded to the nearest hundred thousand.

Year	1920	1930	1940	1950	1960	1970	1980	1990
Population (in millions)	10.4	12.6	13.5	14.8	16.8	18.2	17.6	18.0

On a separate sheet of graph paper, draw a graph showing the growth in population in New York State from 1920 to 1990. Use the graph in Activity 44 as a model.

Answer the questions about the population of New York. Show your work where necessary.

1. The 1990 population was approximately _____ times that of 1920.

2. Fill in the table for each decade. Write whether the population increased or decreased. Use approximate numbers to estimate the percent change.

Proportion: $\dfrac{\text{Amount of change}}{\text{Base year population}} = \dfrac{\text{Percent change}}{100}$

Decade	Increase or decrease	Amount of change	Percent change
1920–1930			
1960–1970			
1970–1980			
1980–1990			

J. Weston Walch, Publisher

Name _____ Date _____

ACTIVITY 45 ■ *(continued)*

3. In the period 1920–1990, the population of California grew from 3.4 million to 29.8 million. Compare the population growth in California with that of New York.

Think about this:

1. What do these population figures tell you about New York?

2. Economists talk about "negative growth." What do you think it means? Give an example.

3. Analyze the growth in the population of your city or state.

J. Weston Walch, Publisher

Name _____   Date _____

ACTIVITY 46 ■ Big Money

The bar graph shows the amount of money that a certain country included in its military budget for each year.

Answer these questions about the graph:

1. It includes the years

   _____ to _____ .

2. The number 200 on the vertical

   scale represents _____ .

3. Measure the bars for each year, in inches or centimeters.

   1980: _____ ;

   1986: _____ .

   The amount for 1986 is about

   _____ times that for 1980.

4. Write as a numeral the approximate amount for each year.

   1980: ___$140,000,000,000___

   1982: _____

   1984: _____

   1986: _____

   1988: _____

   1990: _____

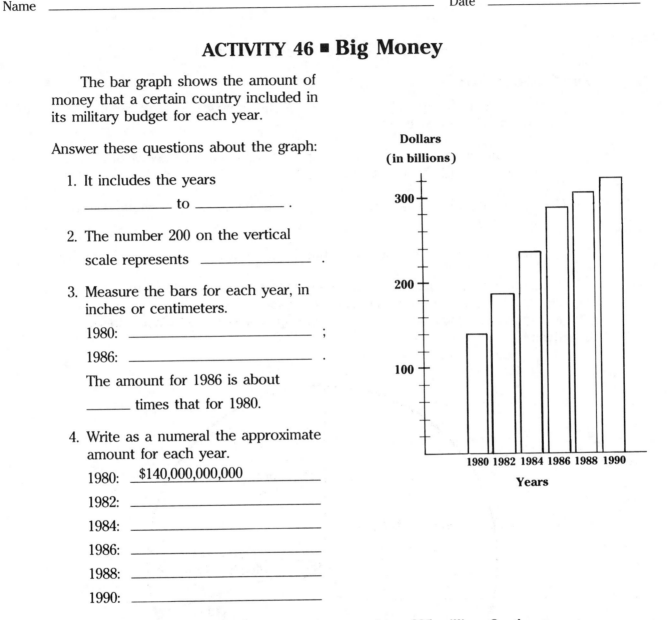

**Dollars
(in billions)**

300

200

100

1980 1982 1984 1986 1988 1990

Years

5. In 1984 the population of the country was about 235 million. On the average, how much did each person pay for military purposes that year? Write the numbers that you use to find the answer mentally.

J. Weston Walch, Publisher

Name _____   Date _____

ACTIVITY 46 ■ *(continued)*

Think about this:

1. This circle graph, also called a "pie chart," shows how large a piece of the pie was allotted to each item.

   (a) Estimate the measure in degrees, of each piece, called a *sector* of the circle. A complete circle measures 360°.

   (b) The total budget was $625 billion. Estimate the amount of money allotted to each item.

   (c) How can you check that your estimates are reasonable?

2. Some people think that we need a large military budget to keep the country strong. Other people would prefer that we spend less for military purposes and more for education, health care, and other social needs. What do you think?

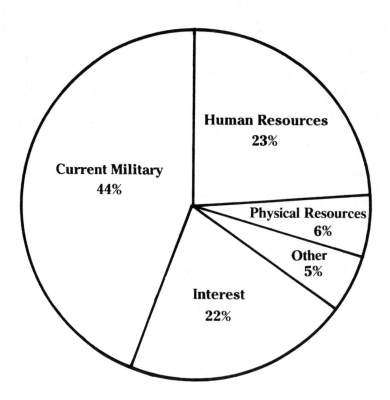

J. Weston Walch, Publisher

Name _____   Date _____

ACTIVITY 47 ▪ Where Does the Money Go?

Governments spend a great deal of money. For a certain year the president proposed a budget of $925 billion. This circle graph shows how the president planned to spend the money.

1. Use the approximate numbers to estimate *mentally* the amount of money to be spent for each item. You may want to use this "ratio" method. (≈ means "approximately equal to")

   (a) Ratios. Interest: 12%

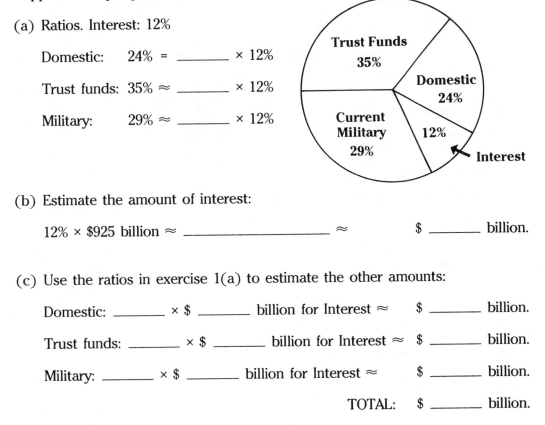

   Domestic: 24% = _____ × 12%

   Trust funds: 35% ≈ _____ × 12%

   Military: 29% ≈ _____ × 12%

   (b) Estimate the amount of interest:

   12% × $925 billion ≈ _____ ≈ $ _____ billion.

   (c) Use the ratios in exercise 1(a) to estimate the other amounts:

   Domestic: _____ × $ _____ billion for Interest ≈ $ _____ billion.

   Trust funds: _____ × $ _____ billion for Interest ≈ $ _____ billion.

   Military: _____ × $ _____ billion for Interest ≈ $ _____ billion.

                                              TOTAL: $ _____ billion.

   (d) Check: Is the total close to $925 billion? Give your opinion of "close to":

   between $ _____ billion and $ _____ billion.

J. Weston Walch, Publisher

Name _____   Date _____

ACTIVITY 47 ▪ *(continued)*

2. Compute the amount to be spent for each item, using the percents in the circle diagram and the total budget figure of $925 billion. Round to the nearest billion dollars. You may want to use a calculator. Show necessary work on another sheet of paper.

    Interest: $ _____ billion   Military: $ _____ billion

    Domestic: $ _____ billion   Total: $ _____ billion

    Trust funds: $ _____ billion

Write the difference between the correct figure and your estimate, in billions of dollars, for each item:

    Interest: _____ ;   Trust funds: _____ ;

    Domestic: _____ ;   Military: _____ .

Think about this:

Trust funds, 35% of the budget, are mostly for Social Security. The government holds this money "in trust" to give back to people when they grow older and no longer work. Many people think that these funds should be kept separate from the annual budget. On another sheet calculate the budget with trust funds omitted: total amount, and percent for each item. Draw a circle graph.

J. Weston Walch, Publisher

CHAPTER 5

Fun with Math

Activities 48–58

This chapter introduces several areas of mathematics that students may not have encountered in the standard curriculum. They will learn about the mathematical practices and games of diverse cultures, relating to the topics of graph theory, number theory, map coloring, and logic.

The topics in this chapter are:

Activities 48–51: Magic squares, their origins in Asia and spread to Africa and Europe, construction of 3 × 3 and 4 × 4 squares, finding errors, translation of squares written in East Arabic numerals, and the artist Dürer's magic square.

Activity 52: Secret codes involving numerology of the ancient Greeks and Hebrews.

Activity 53: Map coloring.

Activities 54–56: Networks in African cultures and in our own.

Activities 57 & 58: Three-in-a-row games of the Philippines and the Pueblo Indians of our Southwest.

REQUIRED MATERIALS

Activities 50 & 52: Calculators (optional).

Activity 53: Crayons or colored markers (optional).

Activity 55: Grid paper, crayons or colored markers.

Activity 56: Grid paper.

Activities 57 & 58: Two students play; three counters for each, of two different colors.

Activity 57: Stiff paper or Styrofoam®, art materials (optional).

Name _____ Date _____

ACTIVITY 48 ■ The First Magic Square

The first magic square, called *Lo-Shu*, appeared on the back of a turtle in the River Lo, more than 4,000 years ago. So says an old Chinese myth.

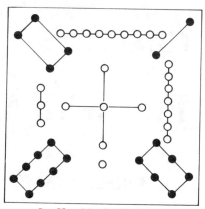

Lo-Shu Magic Square

Each group of connected dots stands for a number. Count all the dots in each row across:

first: _____ ; second _____ ; third: _____ .

Count the dots in each column:

first: _____ ; second _____ ; third: _____ .

Count the dots in each diagonal: _____ , _____ .

This sum, called the *magic sum*, is the same every time. That is why the square is called "magic." People thought that it brought good luck.

Copy the Chinese Lo-Shu in the blank 3 × 3 square, using our Indo-Arabic numerals. What kind of numbers

are shown by black dots? _____ ;

by white dots? _____ .

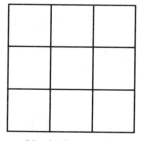

Magic Square A

Complete the magic squares below. Use each of the numbers 1 to 9 exactly once. Be sure to check all eight sums in each square.

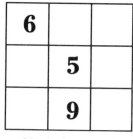

Magic Square B

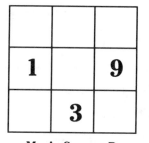

Magic Square C

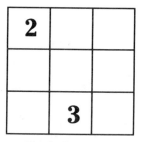

Magic Square D

Magic Square E

J. Weston Walch, Publisher

Name _____ Date _____

ACTIVITY 48 ■ *(continued)*

Complete the sentences below about the magic squares on the previous page:

1. The magic sum is _____ .

2. The number in the center is _____ .

3. The numbers in the corners are _____ numbers.

4. Rotate Magic Square A (Lo-Shu) a half a turn (180°). The new square is the
   same as Magic Square _____ .

Think about this:

1. There are eight different magic squares using the numbers from 1 to 9. You
   have already made five. Can you make the other three?

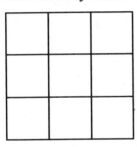 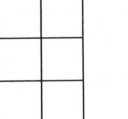 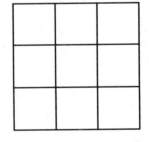

2. Think of a number. Add this number to every number in a magic square. Is
   the result a magic square? Show some examples.

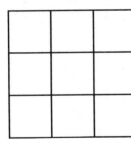 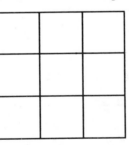 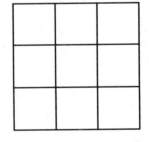

3. Think of a number. Multiply every number of a magic square by this number.
   Is the result a magic square? Show some examples.

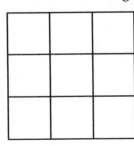 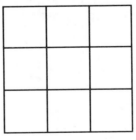 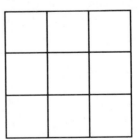

J. Weston Walch, Publisher

Name _____   Date _____

ACTIVITY 49 ■ Magic Squares: Find the Mistake

A magic square is a square array of numbers arranged in a special way:

- No number may be used more than once.
- The sum of every row (add across), every column (add up or down), and each of the two diagonals is the same number, called the *magic sum*.

Complete this magic square. The magic sum is 15. Be sure to check all eight sums.

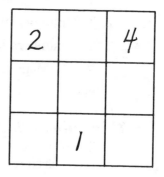

Magic squares spread from China to India and Japan, to the Middle East, to Africa, and finally to Europe and America. In the Middle East and Africa they became part of Islam, the religion of the Muslims. These magic squares are written in East Arabic numerals. Finish translating them. The magic sum is 15.

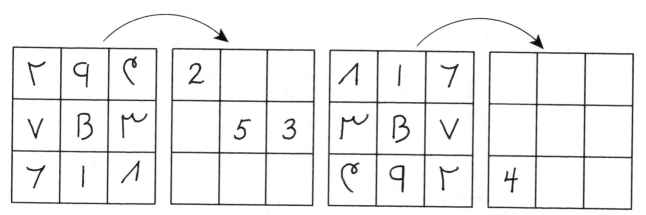

Muslim wise men formed more and more complicated squares. They called the construction of magic squares "the science of secrets." To keep ordinary people from learning this science, they would purposely write squares with mistakes. Perhaps they used these squares as a code to send secret messages!

J. Weston Walch, Publisher

Name _____   Date _____

ACTIVITY 49 ■ *(continued)*

Correct the mistake in each magic square:

Magic sum is 12.

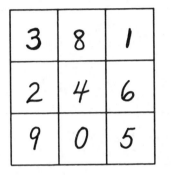

Magic sum is 30.

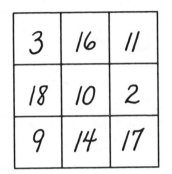

Magic sum is 34.

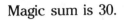

Think about this:

Construct a magic square having a mistake. Ask a friend to correct it. Try to write it in East Arabic numerals.

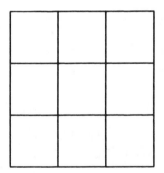

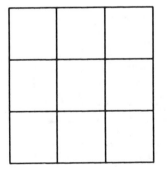

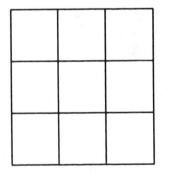

J. Weston Walch, Publisher

Name _____   Date _____

ACTIVITY 50 ■ Four-by-Four Magic Squares

This four-by-four magic square appears in an etching by the German artist Albrecht Dürer. He called the picture *Melancolia*, meaning "sadness." The bottom line shows the year in which the etching was done: 1514.

16	3	2	13
5	10	11	8
9	6	7	12
4	15	14	1

1. Dürer used all the numbers from _____ to

   _____ .

2. The sum of the numbers in every row, every column, and each diagonal is the same, and is called the *magic number*. In this square the magic number is

   _____ .

3. Find the sum of *all* the numbers in each 2 × 2 square:

   Center _____ ; upper left _____ ; lower left _____ ; upper right

   _____ ; lower right _____ .

4. Here is one way to construct a 4 × 4 magic square with the numbers 1 to 16.

   (a) Start with this array:

1	2	3	4
5	6	7	8
9	10	11	12
13	14	15	16

   (b) Rewrite the numbers in each diagonal in the opposite order.

   (c) Recopy the remaining numbers in the same order as in the original square.

   (d) Check the magic sum.

J. Weston Walch, Publisher

Name _____ Date _____

ACTIVITY 50 ■ *(continued)*

How is this square different from Dürer's?

16	2	3	
	11		
		6	
4			1

Think about this:

This magic square from West Africa has one mistake. You may want to use a calculator to find it.

The mistake is in row _____ , column

_____ .

The number _____ should be _____ .

Explain how you found the mistake.

16	19	22	9
21	12	15	20
11	24	17	14
18	13	12	23

J. Weston Walch, Publisher

Name _____   Date _____

ACTIVITY 51 ▪ More Four-by-Four Magic Squares

1. You can make a magic square with zero and positive and negative numbers. First, complete the table.

+8 + +6 =	–6 + –8 =	–6 + –6 =	+3 – –5 =
–5 – +3 =	–3 + +7 =	0 + +2 =	–2 – 0 =
–4 – –4 =	+3 + –7 =	–10 – –4 =	10 – +4 =
–3 + –7 =	7 + 3 =	4 + 8 =	–8 + –8 =

Transfer each answer to the corresponding space in the large square.

Find the sum of the four numbers in each row, each column, and each diagonal. All ten sums should be the same. If they are not, try to find your errors.

2. Look at any month of a calendar, or imagine how the numbers are arranged. Choose any 4 × 4 square of numbers, and copy the square array. Rearrange the numbers to form a magic square.

Think about this:

Discuss this question with your group: Why can a 4 × 4 square of numbers in a calendar be rearranged to form a magic square? Prove that it always works.

J. Weston Walch, Publisher

Name _____   Date _____

ACTIVITY 52 ■ Secret Codes with Numbers

The ancient Greeks and Hebrews used the letters of their alphabets to write their numerals. People thought that they could predict the future by adding the number values of the letters in a word. This practice was called *Gematria*. It is a form of numerology.

Below each letter is a number. Call this set of numbers *Set N.*

Letters:	A	B	C	D	E	F	G	H	I
Numbers (Set N):	1	2	3	4	5	6	7	8	9

Find the number value of the word BAD: B = 2, A = 1, D = 4.   2 + 1 + 4 = 7

The number 7 is often thought to be unlucky. When the numerologist doesn't like the answer, he or she may use a different set of numbers. For example, the numerologist may assign to each letter the square of the original number. Call the squares *Set S.*

Letters:	A	B	C	D	E	F	G	H	I
Numbers (Set S):	1	4	9	16	25	36	49	64	81

Find the number value of the word BAD, using Set S. BAD = 4 + 1 + 16 = 21. 21 = 3 × 7, three times as unlucky as before!

Write the number value of each word, using both Set N and Set S. Compare the words, and find the easiest method.

Word:	HE	HAD	HEAD	HID	HIDE	CHIDE
Set N:	13					
Set S:	89					

J. Weston Walch, Publisher

Name _____ Date _____

ACTIVITY 52 ■ *(continued)*

Find the word or words represented by the following pairs of numbers. The first line in the chart gives the number of letters in each word. Do your work on a separate sheet of paper. You may want to use a calculator.

Number of letters:	2	3	3	3	4	3	4	3	3
Set N:	7	11	12	14	12	9	15	19	14
Set S:	29	45	54	78	46	35	71	123	98
Word:									

Think about this:

The ancient Hebrews and Greeks continued their system, counting by tens. This is how it would work out in the Latin alphabet that we use.

Letter:	J	K	L	M	N
Numbers (Set N):	10	20	30	40	50
Numbers (Set S):	100	400	900	1600	2500

Think of three words which are spelled with letters from A through N. Write the number of letters in the word, and the number value of the word in both Set N and Set S. Ask a friend to figure out the words.

J. Weston Walch, Publisher

Name _____   Date _____

ACTIVITY 53 ■ Map Coloring

To make map reading easy, the mapmaker uses different colors for two countries that share a common border. At the same time, the mapmaker wants to save money by using as few colors as possible.

Write the number of regions in each map. Write the *smallest* number of colors that can be used to color each map. Let numbers represent the different colors, and write a number in pencil inside each region of the map.

Example: This map has *five* regions. It can be colored with *three* colors.

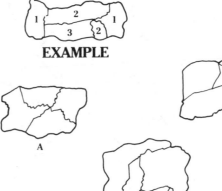

EXAMPLE

Map	Number of Regions	Colors
A		
B		
C		
Southern Africa		

Mathematicians and mapmakers discovered centuries ago that four colors are sufficient to color the most complicated map, but were unable to *prove* that four was *always* the greatest number of colors. A few years ago mathematicians worked out a computer proof of the Four-Color Theorem. In 1987 a 16-year-old high school student, Elizabeth Lee Wilmer, received a Westinghouse award for her original research on maps requiring only three colors.

Think about this:

On another sheet draw a map of ten regions that requires four colors. Ask a friend to color it.

SOUTHERN AFRICA

J. Weston Walch, Publisher

Name _____   Date _____

ACTIVITY 54 ■ Networks (Part 1): Chokwe

Before the time of television, radio, or formal schools, children learned the ways of their people from their parents and grandparents. Among the Chokwe people, who live in the African countries of Zaire, Zambia, and Angola, the village elders taught the children as they sat around the fire at night. They illustrated their stories by drawing *network* patterns in the sand.

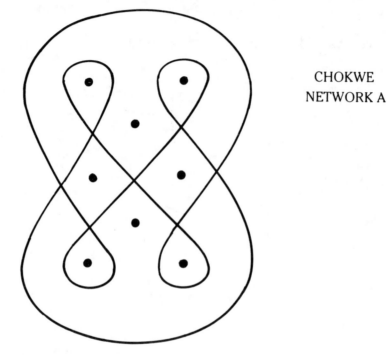

CHOKWE
NETWORK A

Network A is an object that can accompany dancers and send messages. It is

a _____ .

J. Weston Walch, Publisher

Name _____   Date _____

ACTIVITY 54 ■ *(continued)*

Network B illustrates the Chokwe myth of the beginning of the world.

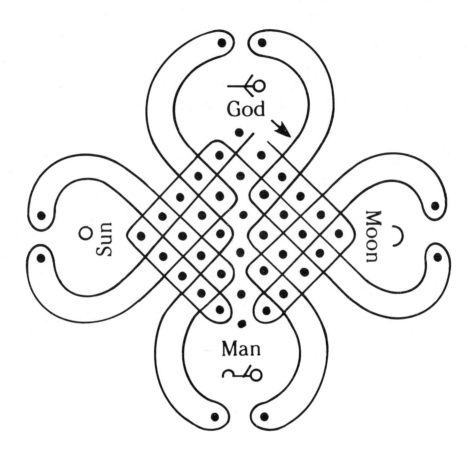

Trace each network without taking your pencil off the paper or going over a line more than once. You may *cross* a line. Such networks are called *traceable* networks. Ignore the dots. The arrow shows you where to start Network B.

Copy the pattern of dots in Network A. Use the dots as a guide to copy Network A. Work on another sheet.

J. Weston Walch, Publisher

Name _____ Date _____

ACTIVITY 54 ■ *(continued)*

Think about this:

Copy Network B in the space below. It may be helpful to follow these steps:

1. Copy the pattern of dots in the central part of the network. How many dots are there? _____ What shape do they form? _____
2. Copy the remaining eight dots.
3. Draw the network, using the dots to guide you.

J. Weston Walch, Publisher

Name _____   Date _____

ACTIVITY 55 ■ Networks (Part 2): Bakuba

The Bakuba people have lived for many centuries in the part of Africa that is now called Zaire. In fact, their historians can recount stories about their kings going back 15 centuries.

Early in the twentieth century Emil Torday, a Belgian anthropologist, lived among the Bakuba (also called Kuba) for some time. One day he saw some young children drawing figures in the sand. They invited him to copy these figures without lifting his finger or going over a line segment more than once. He wrote in his book that these were "impossible tasks." Yet the African children carried them out with no difficulty.

Torday included copies of these figures in his book, the networks you will see in the next activity. But first you will draw and analyze simpler figures of the same type.

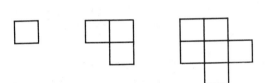

1. Here are some networks of that type, each larger than the one before.

   (a) Use a pencil to trace each figure without lifting the pencil off the paper or going over a line segment more than once. Where do you start the network? Where do you finish? Mark each starting and finishing point. Can they be interchanged?

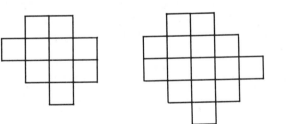

   (b) On a sheet of graph paper, copy each of the networks. Then continue by drawing larger and larger networks. Mark each starting point and finishing point. Can you draw a network that has eight small squares in the longest row?

J. Weston Walch, Publisher

Name _____   Date _____

ACTIVITY 55 ■ *(continued)*

2. Count the small squares in each network. This may get boring by the time you get to the larger figures. See whether you can find a short cut by noticing the number pattern. Write your answers in the table. In the column labeled "Difference," write the difference between the two numbers in the "Total" column.

   What pattern did you discover?

NUMBER OF SMALL SQUARES

Longest Row	Total	Difference
1	1	⟩ 2
2	3	⟩ 3
3	6	⟩
4		
5		
6		
7		
8		

Think about this:

1. Color your networks to make the patterns more interesting.

2. Describe the starting and finishing points of the networks. You may want to use diagrams. Then exchange your description with a classmate. After reading your classmate's description, would you know exactly where to start each network from that description?

J. Weston Walch, Publisher

Name _____   Date _____

ACTIVITY 56 ■ Networks (Part 3): More Bakuba

Along the Kasai River, in Zaire, live the Bakuba people. They are famous for the beautiful patterns in their weaving and woodcarving. Children trace these *network* designs in the sand, in imitation of their parents' woven cloth and fishing nets.

Trace each network without taking your pencil off the paper or going over a line more than once. You may *cross* a line. A network which can be traced in this way is called a *traceable* network.

Both networks are traceable. However, you must be sure to start at the right point. Each network has two points that are "right." If you start at one of these points, you will finish at the other.

How are the starting and finishing points different from any other points where lines intersect?

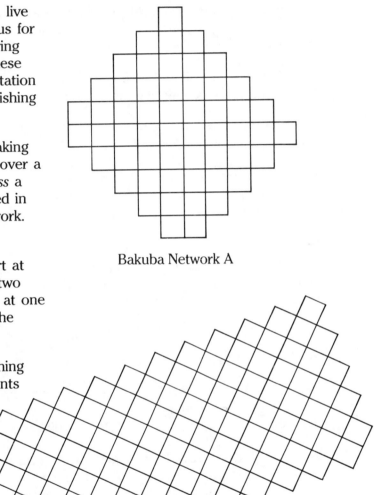

Bakuba Network A

Bakuba Network B

Think about this:

1. On a sheet of graph paper draw a network similar to one on this page, but having more small squares.

2. Give some examples of networks in our culture.

J. Weston Walch, Publisher

Name _____   Date _____

ACTIVITY 57 ■ Three-in-a-Row Games: Tapatan

People around the world play three-in-a-row games, similar to Tic-Tac-Toe. Two people play against each other. The first player to place three of his or her markers in a straight row is the winner.

This version, called Tapatan, comes from the Philippines. You may draw the "game board" on a sheet of paper. You will need:

COUNTERS: Three for each player, of two different colors, like white and black.

GAME BOARD: Copy this diagram. The game is played on the nine points where the lines meet.

RULES:

Stage 1. The two players take turns going first. Player One places a white counter on any point. Then Player Two places a black counter on any empty point. They take turns until all the counters have been placed on the game board.

Stage 2. Player One moves any white counter along a line to the next empty point. Jumping over a counter is not allowed. Player Two does the same with any black counter. They continue to take turns moving their counters.

OBJECT OF THE GAME: Each player tries to make a row of three counters of his or her color, and to block the other player from making a row. A row can be made horizontally, vertically, or along a diagonal.

END OF THE GAME: The first person to make a row is the winner. If neither player can get three counters in a row, the game is a draw. The game ends in a draw when the same set of moves has been repeated three times.

Think about this:

1. After you have played the game several times, analyze your strategy. Where should the first player place the first counter? Is the person who goes first more likely to win than the second player? Discuss with your partner the best strategy to follow. Write down the steps. Then see whether it works out in practice.

2. Make a game board of stiff paper or Styrofoam®. Decorate it with Philippine flags or other appropriate symbols.

    J. Weston Walch, Publisher

Name _____ Date _____

ACTIVITY 58 ■ Three-in-a-Row Games: Picaría

The Spanish king, Alfonso the Wise, is the author of the first book of games written in Europe. Many of the games in this thirteenth-century book were brought to Spain by the Arabic-speaking Moors of North Africa. One of these games, called *Alquerque*, has many different versions. An illustration in the *Book of Games* shows two children playing *Alquerque de Tres*, a three-in-a-row game.

Early in the twentieth century, Stewart Culin wrote a book called *Games of the North American Indians*. In this book he described a similar game called *Picaría*, played by Pueblo children of New Mexico. Perhaps they learned it from the Spanish settlers. Although the Pueblo Indians fought hard against the Spanish rulers, they may have adopted Spanish games.

Unfortunately Culin did not give the exact rules for the game. Did they play on a game board with nine points or thirteen points? Here are both versions. You may decide which is a better game. Two people play.

COUNTERS: Three for each player, of two different colors, like white and black.

GAME BOARD: Copy this diagram on a large sheet of paper. The game is played on the nine marked points.

RULES: The two players take turns placing one counter at a time on an empty point on the board. When all six counters have been put down, the players take turns moving one counter at a time along any line to the next empty point. Jumping over a counter is not allowed.

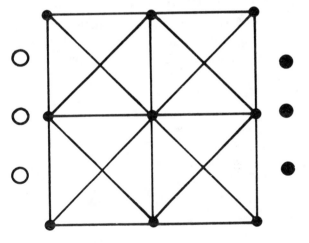

OBJECT OF THE GAME: Each player tries to make a row of three counters of his or her color, and to block the other player from making a row. A row can be made horizontally, vertically, or along a diagonal.

END OF THE GAME: The first person to make a row is the winner. If neither player can get three in a row and the game becomes boring, call it a draw.

J. Weston Walch, Publisher

Name _____   Date _____

ACTIVITY 58 ■ *(continued)*

CHANGE THE RULES

Some people play Picaría on the thirteen points marked on this game board. Follow the rules for the nine-point version, but with these differences:

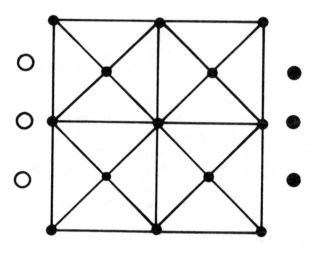

1. Neither player may place a counter in the center of the board until all six counters are on the board.

2. You may make a row of three anywhere along a diagonal, as long as there is no empty point between two counters in the row. A row can be made in sixteen different ways.

Think about this:

Discuss with your partner which version you both prefer. Think about the challenge of each version, how long it takes to finish a game, whether the person who starts is more likely to win, and any other factors you can think of. Write your conclusions, and discuss them with the class. Do the other students agree with you?

J. Weston Walch, Publisher

Bibliography for Multicultural and Global Mathematics

Books and Articles for Adults

Dolber, Sam. *From Recreation to Computation Around the World.* San Carlos, CA: Math Products Plus, 1980. A collection of historical and multicultural enrichment activities, as well as several board games, with reproducible game boards.

Grunfeld, Frederic, ed. *Games of the World.* NY: Ballantine Books, 1977. Beautifully illustrated in full color, this book describes the origins of over a hundred games, with instructions for making and playing them.

Janvier, Claude. "Contextualization and mathematics for all." In Thomas J. Cooney, *Teaching and Learning Mathematics in the 1990s* (1990 Yearbook), Reston, VA: National Council of Teachers of Mathematics (NCTM): 183–193. The importance of placing mathematics education in a context that is meaningful to the students.

Joseph, George C. *The Crest of the Peacock: Non-European Roots of Mathematics.* London: I. B. Tauris, 1991. Distributed in the U.S. by St. Martin's Press, NY. Well-illustrated history, generally neglected until now.

Krause, Marina C. *Multicultural Mathematics Materials.* Reston, VA: NCTM, 1983. Mathematical games and activies from around the world, designed to enhance students' ethnic identity and to help them to appreciate the ethnic heritage of others.

Russ, Laurence M. *Mancala Games.* Algonac, MI: Reference Publications, 1984. Rules for playing many variations of this excellent game of strategy, known as *ayo, oware, adi, bao,* etc., in its African versions.

Schwartz, Richard H. *Mathematics and Global Survival.* Needham, MA: Ginn, 1990. Many exercises that highlight the relevance of mathematics to global and environmental issues. Easily adaptable to the middle grades.

Zaslavsky, Claudia. *Africa Counts: Number and Pattern in African Culture.* Brooklyn, NY: Lawrence Hill Books, 1979. Well-illustrated discussion of African numeration systems, everyday uses and mystical attributes of numbers, geometry in art and architecture, and mathematical games.

_____. "Symmetry and other mathematical concepts in African life." In *Applications in School Mathematics* (1979 Yearbook). Reston, VA: NCTM.

_____. "Bringing the world into the math class." *Curriculum Review* 24 (Jan.–Feb. 1985): 62–65. How teachers can encourage an awareness of the role of mathematics in everyday life by looking at numeration, measurement, games, and architecture in various societies.

————. Articles published in the *Arithmetic Teacher* (NCTM):

"Networks—New York subways, a piece of string, and African traditions." 29, 2 (October 1981): 42–47.

"People who live in round houses." 37, 1 (September 1989): 18–21.

"Symmetry in American folk art." 38, 1 (September 1990): 6–12.

"Multicultural mathematics education for the middle grades." 38, 6 (February 1991): 8–13.

Books for Young People

Arnold, Arnold. *The World Book of Children's Games.* World Publishing, 1972. One chapter is devoted to number games. Another chapter describes games of strategy of various cultures and includes excellent background material.

Lumpkin, Beatrice. *Senefer and Hatshepsut.* Trenton, NJ: Africa World Press, 1992. A novel highlighting the mathematical achievements of ancient Egypt.

Miles, Betty. *Save the Earth: An Action Handbook for Kids.* NY: Knopf, 1991. Encourages young people to think globally and act locally about many issues. Suggested activities lend themselves to mathematical treatment.

St. John, Glory. *How to Count Like a Martian.* NY: Walck, 1975. Introduction to many numeration systems in the context of a mystery story.

Zaslavsky, Claudia. *TIC TAC TOE and Other Three-in-a-Row Games, from Ancient Egypt to the Modern Computer.* NY: Crowell, 1982. For each version, the book presents a brief history, rules of play, tips on how to be a good player, and suggestions for variations.

Other Resources

Dover Publications publishes many books on ethnic art, patterns, and games.

Metropolitan Museum of Art, New York, NY. "The Mathematics of Islamic Art" (1979). Kit of materials includes 20 full-color slides and a transparency, enabling students to construct the repeating geometric patterns characteristic of Islamic art.

"Multicultural Mathematics Posters and Activities." Reston, VA: NCTM, 1984. Kit includes 18 attractive posters, an activity book that emphasizes problem solving, and many references.

Answer Key

Activity 1

	Words	Explanation	Operations
43	forty-three	four times ten plus three	multiply, add
18	eighteen	eight plus ten	add
79	seventy-nine	seven times ten plus nine	multiply, add
21	twenty-one	two times ten plus one	multiply, add
403	four hundred three	four times a hundred plus three	multiply, add
5060	five thousand sixty	five times a thousand plus six times ten	multiply, add

1. twenty   4. fifty

2. twenty-five   5. twenty-nine

3. ninety   6. thirty-five

Think About This (TAT): 1. probably because counting began with finger counting

Activity 2

1. 2, 20, 28, 206, 1000s, 44

2.

Standard	Egyptian	Roman (Ancient)	Roman (Modern)
54	∩∩∩∩∩ IIII	LIIII	LIV
128	⟨ ∩∩ IIII/IIII	CXXVIII	CXXVIII
204	⟨⟨ IIII	CCIIII	CCIV
1090	𐤀 ∩∩∩∩/∩∩∩∩∩	MLXXXX	MXC

4. 4, 20, 12, 9, 12

5. Egyptian, Ancient Roman

6. Standard, Maya

TAT: Most people in the world use standard numerals because they require few symbols, and they make calculations easy (see Activity 4).

J. Weston Walch, Publisher

Activity 3

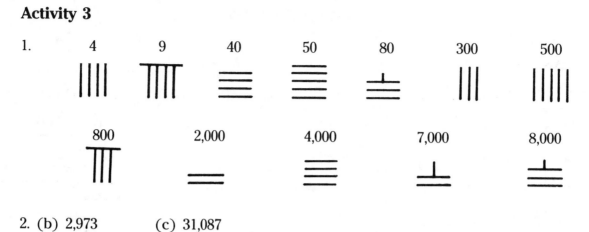

1.   4   9   40   50   80   300   500

    800   2,000   4,000   7,000   8,000

2. (b) 2,973   (c) 31,087

3. Students check their answers.

4. (a)   (b)   (c)   (d)

TAT: 1. Alike: Place value (positional notation), base 10, highest value on the left.
        Different: We use the same set of digits in each position; the stick numerals have the same set of digits in alternate positions.

        2. Students compare their lists.

Activity 4

1. (a) LXXXIV   (b) CCCXX

2. (a) XXI   (b) XLIII

3. (a) 99 ∩∩∩ ∩∩∩ ||| (b) 99   (c) ∩∩∩ ||||

4. (a)   (b)

Activity 5

1. From the top: 8, 12, 14, 8, 15

2. (a) 174   (b) 132   (c) 309   (d) 385

3. (a) 2,369   (b) 3,738   (c) 6,009   (d) 5,383

TAT: 1,243,615 days; the year 292 in our calendar.

J. Weston Walch, Publisher

Activity 6

1.　✓1　　　　13 ✓
　　✓2　　　　26 ✓
　　✓4　　　　52 ✓
　　――　　　　――
　　　7　　　　91

✓ I	∩ III	✓
✓ II	∩∩ III	✓
✓ IIII	∩∩∩∩∩ II	✓
III / IIII	∩∩∩∩∩ ∩∩∩∩ I	

2.

✓ I	∩∩ IIII	✓
✓ II	∩∩∩∩∩ IIII	✓
IIII	𐦀 IIII	
✓ IIII / IIII	𐦀𐦀 ∩ III	✓
IIIII / IIIII I	𐦀𐦀 ∩∩∩∩ IIII IIII	
∩ I	𐦀𐦀 ∩∩∩ IIII III	

✓1　　　　27 ✓
✓2　　　　54 ✓
　4　　　　108
✓8　　　　216 ✓
――　　　　――
　11　　　　297

(simplified)

Activity 7

1. (a) 10, 2, 8
　　(b) 6, 5, 4, 2
　　(c) Decimal point; no.
　　(d) Easy to count beads.

2.　　369.4　　　　　2,301.6　　　　　5,004.02

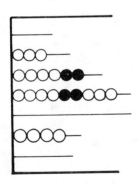

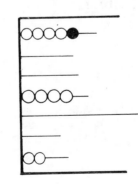

J. Weston Walch, Publisher

Activity 8

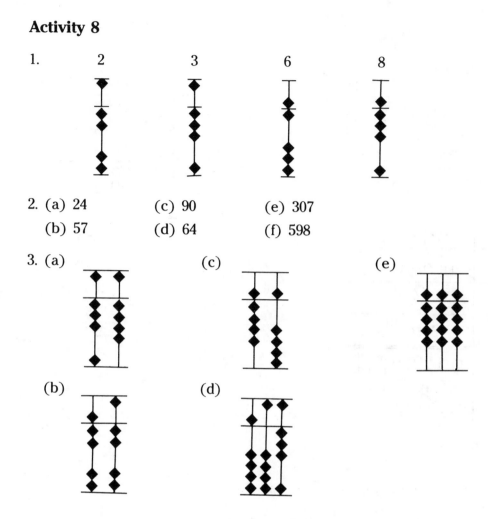

1.   2   3   6   8

2. (a) 24   (c) 90   (e) 307
   (b) 57   (d) 64   (f) 598

3. (a)   (c)   (e)

   (b)   (d)

5. Shortcut: treat 4 as 5 minus 1, and 9 as 10 minus 1.

Activity 9

1. $\frac{1}{15}$

2. $\frac{1}{2} + \frac{1}{6}$

3. $\frac{1}{6} + \frac{1}{18}$ or $\frac{1}{5} + \frac{1}{45}$

4. $\frac{1}{64}$

5. $\frac{1}{2} + \frac{1}{4}$ $\frac{1}{4} + \frac{1}{8}$

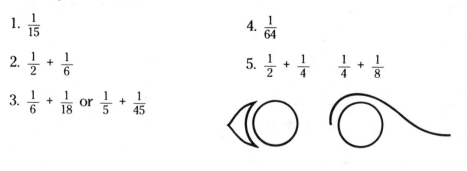

J. Weston Walch, Publisher

Activity 10

1. (b) $\frac{9}{16}$ (d) $\frac{9}{32}$ (f) $\frac{33}{64}$

   (c) $\frac{3}{16}$ (e) $\frac{13}{16}$ (g) $\frac{27}{64}$

2. (a) $\frac{1}{64}$ (c) 1

   (b) squared numbers   (d) A: $\frac{3}{4}$, B: $\frac{7}{8}$, C: $\frac{15}{16}$, D: $\frac{31}{32}$.

Activity 11

1. (a) $\frac{2}{7} = \frac{1}{4} + \frac{1}{28}$ $\frac{2}{11} = \frac{1}{6} + \frac{1}{66}$

   (b) The fraction could be reduced to a unit fraction.

   (c) $\frac{2}{9} = \frac{1}{5} + \frac{1}{45}$ $\frac{2}{15} = \frac{1}{8} + \frac{1}{120}$

2. (b) Easy to divide an even number by 2.

   (c) $\frac{2}{27} = \frac{1}{18} + \frac{1}{54}$ $\frac{2}{33} = \frac{1}{22} + \frac{1}{66}$

TAT: 1. $\frac{2}{5} = \frac{1}{3} + \frac{1}{15}$ Multiply each denominator by 5.

      $\frac{2}{25} = \frac{1}{13} + \frac{1}{325}$

Activity 12

	A	B	C	D
340	three hundred forty	34	thirty-four	N
3.40	three and forty-hundredths	3.4	three and four-tenths	N
0.34	thirty-four hundredths	.34	thirty-four hundredths	H
304	three hundred four	34	thirty-four	N
03.4	three and four-tenths	3.4	three and four-tenths	U
.034	thirty-four thousandths	.34	thirty-four hundredths	N
034	thirty-four	34	thirty-four	U
.340	three hundred forty thousandths	.34	thirty-four hundredths	N
34.0	thirty-four and zero tenths	34	thirty-four	N

J. Weston Walch, Publisher

Activity 12 *(continued)*

TAT: 1. (a) 2,005; 5,020; 5.002; 2.500, etc.

(b) 0.205; 0.250, etc.

(c) 025.0; 0502; 05.20, etc.

2. It is not a place-value system, and a place holder is not necessary.

Activity 13

1. 2,689, 7; 6,383, 2; 3,060, 0

2. (a) 1, correct

(b) 2, 3,098;

(c) 3, ?

(d) 0, 39,618

TAT: 1. 4,674, 3

2. Both the correct answer and the incorrect answer have the same digital.

Activity 14

1. 5, 7, 11, 13, 17, 19

2.

Even numbers	Number of ways
4 = 2 + 2	1
6 = 3 + 3	1
8 = 3 + 5	1
10 = 3 + 7 or 5 + 5	2
12 = 5 + 7	1
14 = 7 + 7 or 3 + 11	2
16 = 3 + 13 or 5 + 11	2
18 = 5 + 13 or 7 + 11	2
20 = 3 + 17 or 7 + 13	2

3. Two is the only even prime number. If 2 is one addend, the other addend must be even, and not prime.

J. Weston Walch, Publisher

Activity 14 *(continued)*

TAT: Even number: <u>22   24   26   28   30</u>

Number of ways: <u>3   3   3   2   3</u>

No pattern

Activity 15

1. $c = 5$ cm.
2. $b = 6$ ft.
4. a is odd; $c = b + 1$; $a^2 = b + c$

a	b	c	$a^2 \ + \ b^2 \overset{?}{=} c^2$
3	4	5	9 + 16 = 25
5	12	13	25 + 144 = 169
7	24	25	49 + 576 = 625
9	40	41	81 + 1600 = 1681
11	60	61	121 + 3600 = 3721
13	84	85	169 + 7056 = 7225

TAT: 1.

a	b	c	a^2	+	b^2	$\overset{?}{=}$	c^2
60	45	75	3,600	+	2,025	=	5,625
72	65	97	5,184	+	4,225	=	9,409
3456	3367	4825	11,943,936	+	11,336,689	=	23,280,625

2. 4:3:5; multiply each number by 15.

J. Weston Walch, Publisher

Activity 16

	(1) Exact number	(2) Nearest hundred	(3) Nearest thousand	(4) Two significant figures
	349,621	349,600	350,000	350,000
	483,450	483,500	483,000	480,000
	24,389	24,400	24,000	24,000
	158,460	158,500	158,000	160,000
	29,642	29,600	30,000	30,000
	983	1,000	1,000	980
	300,206	300,200	300,000	300,000
Sums	513,680	513,700	513,000	514,980

20, 680, 1300; columns 1 and 4

1. E	4. E	7. A
2. A	5. A	8. A
3. A	6. E	

Activity 17

Answers may vary. The numbers below were rounded to two significant figures.

Chen	15,000,000	fifteen million
Lopez	14,000,000	fourteen million
Rodman	1,000,000	one million
TOTAL	63,000,000	sixty-three million
Bilsky	1,300,000	one million three hundred thousand
Perone	500,000	five hundred thousand
Jones	20,000	twenty thousand
TOTAL	1,800,000	one million eight hundred thousand

National: 1 or 4, possibly 2

State: 3 or 4; the numbers have fewer places than in the national.

TAT: Errors are due to rounding.

J. Weston Walch, Publisher

Activity 18

Bunch: 200 shells; head: 2,000 shells

1. 175
2. 290
3. 1,730
4. 4,665
5. 13,120
6. 34,920

TAT: About 100,000; about 5 million; 5,110,000

Activity 19

40; 2,000; 10

1. 4,820
2. 3,128; 2,320
3. Answers will vary.

TAT: 1. Possible answers: A bag was as much as a person could carry; a cocoa bean is heavier than a cowrie shell; both cowries and cocoa beans had other uses.

2. $8,000 = 20^3$

Activity 20

1.   (a) 1,440
     (b) 168
     (c) 10,080
     (d) 8,760 (except leap year)
     (e) 525,600

2. Answers will vary.

TAT: About one-fifth

Activity 21

Answers will vary.

Activity 22

Houston	1,200,000	1,600,000	+400,000	+33%
New York	7,900,000	7,100,000	–800,000	–10%
Washington	760,000	640,000	–120,000	–16%

TAT: Amount: Washington, Anchorage, Houston, New York
        Rate: New York, Washington, Houston, Anchorage
The base (1970 population) is different in each case.

J. Weston Walch, Publisher

Activity 23

1900	76	45	145%
1940	132	56	74%
1980	227	95	72%

The rate of increase became smaller, while the amount of increase grew larger.

TAT: 1. 217 million, 2170%, 23, $\frac{1}{23}$

2. Approximately 19, 28, 54, 56

Activity 24

1. $280,000,000,000
2. About $1200
3. $5.4 billion, $770 million, $32,000,000, $530,000
4. 3,000,000,000,000; about $12,000 to $13,000

TAT: About 12,000 times

Activity 25

6 m, almost 12 m

B	5 m	35 m²
C	4 m	32 m²
D	2 m	20 m²
E	$\frac{1}{2}$ m	$5 \frac{3}{4}$ m²

Largest: 36, 6, 6; square

Area = length × width

TAT: 1. Inuit (Eskimo), Native Americans, rural societies in many countries.

2. Use one pair of sticks of equal size for the width, and another pair for the length, thus forming a parallelogram. Then make sure that the diagonals are of equal length, to form a rectangle.

J. Weston Walch, Publisher

Activity 26

2. Areas: circle—about 80; square—64. Circle is largest.

3. (a) Form a circle with the string. Mark a few points, then draw the circle freehand.

   (b) If the fraction is larger than half, consider it a whole square. If it is less than half, ignore it.

   (c) Use symmetry. Count the squares in one quarter of the circle, then multiply by four.

   TAT: Inuit igloo, Native American tipi, Zulu homes, etc.

Activity 27

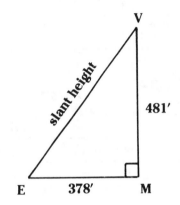

1. 2.6 tons

3. $\overline{EV}$ = 612 ft.

   Area of face = $\frac{1}{2} \times 756 \times 612$

   $\quad\quad\quad\quad\quad\quad = 231,336$ sq. ft.

   $\overline{VM}^2 = (481)^2 = 231,361$

Activity 28

1. Ratio = 1.6; yes.

2. A: 6.4 cm, B: 24 cm, C: 5.6 m, D: 20 ft

3. E: 2.0 cm, F: 25 in., G: 6 ft

4. 34, 55, 89, 144   (a) 1.60   (b–g) 1.62

TAT: 612/378 = 1.62

Activity 29

1. 2

2. $\frac{9}{16} = \frac{3}{8} + \frac{3}{16}$

3. $2\frac{1}{4} = 1\frac{1}{2} + \frac{3}{4}$

4. 4

Activity 30

1. 32, 48, 24, 208; 4 times

2. Small: 8, 3, 24, 24
   Large: 32, 6, 192, 192
   Ratio: 8 times

3. Surface area: 54 sq. in., 6 sq. in., 9 to 1
   Volume: 27 cu. in., 1 cu. in., 27 to 1

J. Weston Walch, Publisher

Activity 31

Continue the patterns.

Activity 32

Follow the directions.

Activity 33

(a)	(b)	(c)	(d)	(e)	(f)	(g)
1	1	0	5	2	1	1
1	1	2	5	2	1	1

Activity 34

(b)	(c)	(d)
4	infinite number	0
4	infinite number	4

Activity 35

2. (a) hexagon, 5

   (b) Congruent equilateral triangles; each angle measures 60°.

   (c) Six-pointed star

Activity 36

1. Equilateral triangle, rhombus (diamond), six-pointed star, hexagon
2. (a & b) 60° and 120°   (c) 120°

Activity 37

Answers will vary. If several students combine their results, the final probabilities are more likely to be close to the expected values than in the individual cases.

TAT: 1. In general, the larger the number of tosses, the closer the success fraction to 0.5

2. $\frac{1}{4}$, $\frac{1}{2}$, $\frac{1}{4}$

J. Weston Walch, Publisher

Activity 38

Students should compare their results.

TAT: 2. 8 groups. The diagram has three positions: top, middle, bottom. Each position can be filled in one of two ways, with a solid line or a broken line. $2 \times 2 \times 2 = 2^3 = 8$

Activity 39

1. $2^4 = 16$

2. $\frac{1}{16}, \frac{1}{4}, \frac{3}{8}, \frac{1}{4}, \frac{1}{16}$

3. Sum = 1

4. The total number of arrangements is 16. The total number of outcomes is 16.

$\frac{16}{16} = 1$

5. $\frac{1}{2}, \frac{1}{2}$ Equally likely to win or lose.

TAT: 1. $2^5 = 32$. See explanation, Activity 38, TAT, exercise 2.

2. $2^6 = 64$. See answer to Activity 38, TAT, exercise 2.

3. $2^8 = 256$. There are eight half-shells, and each can fall in two ways, up or down.

Activity 40

2. 1½ oz, 210 calories, 4½ g protein, 43½ g carbohydrates, 4½ g fat, 495 g sodium

3. (a)

	HEALTH BREAD	**GREAT BREAD**
Serving size	2 slices	1½ slices
Calories	120	105
Carbohydrates	20 grams	18 grams
Fat	2 grams	1½ grams
Sodium	240 mg	203 mg

(b) Health Bread; Great Bread; smaller amount of each ingredient and fewer calories

J. Weston Walch, Publisher

Activity 41

2. (a) 188,000; 424,000

   (b) 1¾; 5

   (c) Men in 1965; women in 1988

   (d) Men cut down more, but fewer women smoked in the first place.

3. (a) $9,000,000

   (b) $19,000,000

   (c) $178,000,000

Activity 42

1.

	Percent	Degrees
Smoking	64%	230°
Alcohol	15%	54°
Car accidents	7%	25°
AIDS	5%	18°
Suicide and homicide	8%	29°
Drugs	1%	4°

Activity 43

1. Kenya and South Africa; Japan
2. Australia, France, Japan
3. 7, 7, 1½, ½
4. 9.1 per 1,000, slightly smaller than the 1988 rate.

J. Weston Walch, Publisher

Activity 43 *(continued)*

5.

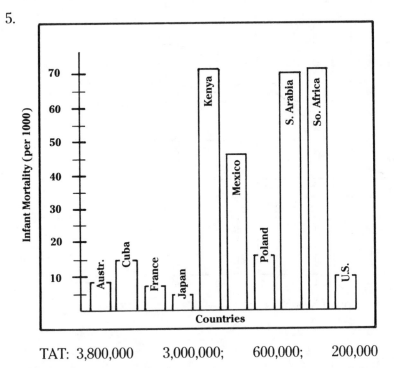

TAT: 3,800,000   3,000,000;   600,000;   200,000

Possible reasons for higher death rate of black infants: higher proportion of poor people among blacks; many do not have health insurance and cannot afford proper health care; low-cost or free health services are not available.

Activity 44

1. 6, 7, 11, 16, 20, 23 (in millions)

2. 22 million, 12 million

3. 8, 2

4. 1950–1960; 5 million

5. 4; 20%

6. 4 million, 25%

7. (b) 30 million

   (d) 7 million, 30%

TAT: 1. Answers will vary, but may include: a late start, favorable climate, job possibilities.

J. Weston Walch, Publisher

Activity 45

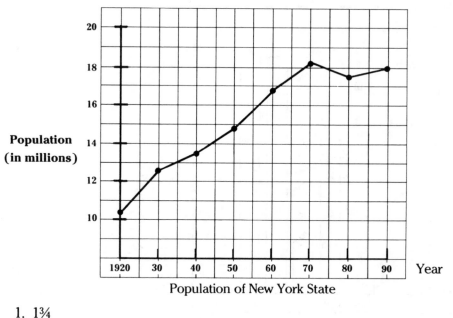

Population of New York State

1. 1¾

2.

increase	2,200,000	21%
increase	1,400,000	8%
decrease	600,000	3%
increase	400,000	2%

3. Cal: 9 times as large.   N.Y.: 1¾ times as large.   Population growth in Cal. was 5 times that of N.Y.

TAT: 1. Answers will vary.

2. A decrease, rather than an increase, like New York in the decade 1970–1980.

Activity 46

1. 1980 to 1985

2. 200 billion dollars

3. 2 times

4. 1982: $183,000,000,000   1986: $286,000,000,000   1990: $312,000,000,000
   1984: $235,000,000,000   1988: $304,000,000,000

5. About $1,000

J. Weston Walch, Publisher

Activity 46 *(continued)*

TAT:	1.			
		Military	158°	$275 billion
		Interest	79	138 billion
		Human Res.	83	144 billion
		Phys. Res.	22	38 billion
		Other	18	31 billion

Approximations may vary slightly from the figures above. To check estimates, find the sum in each column. It should not vary much from the correct sum.

Activity 47

1. (d) "Close to" is between 850 and 1000.

2. Interest 111, Domestic 222, Trust 324, Military 268

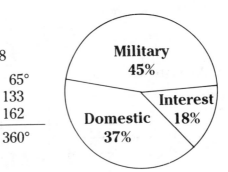

TAT:				
	Interest	$111 billion	18%	65°
	Domestic	222 billion	37	133
	Military	268 billion	45	162
	Total	$600 billion	100%	360°

Activity 48

15 dots; black are even numbers, white are odd numbers.

4	9	2
3	5	7
8	1	6

Magic Square A

6	1	8
7	5	3
2	9	4

Magic Square B

4	3	8
9	5	1
2	7	6

Magic Square C

6	7	2
1	5	9
8	3	4

Magic Square D

2	7	6
9	5	1
4	3	8

Magic Square E

Answers: 15, 5, even, B

J. Weston Walch, Publisher

Activity 48 *(continued)*

TAT: 1.

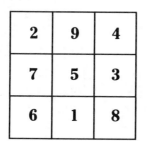

2	9	4
7	5	3
6	1	8

8	3	4
1	5	9
6	7	2

8	1	6
3	5	7
4	9	2

2. The new square is magic.

3. The new square is magic.

Activity 49

2	9	4
7	5	3
6	1	8

8	1	6
3	5	7
4	9	2

The first and second squares are identical.

Mistakes: 9 should be 7; 14 should be 4; 20 should be 10.

TAT: Answers will vary.

Activity 50

1. 1 to 16

2. 34

3. Each sum is 34.

4. Second and third columns are interchanged.

TAT: 2, 2; 12 should be 10.

Activity 51

1.

14	–14	–12	8
–8	4	2	–2
0	–4	–6	6
–10	10	12	–16

Sum = –4

J. Weston Walch, Publisher

Activity 51 *(continued)*

TAT: Proof: Represent the 4 × 4 calendar square:
Rearrange the numbers to form a magic square.
Magic sum is 4n + 48.

n	n + 7	n + 2	n + 3
n + 7	n + 8	n + 9	n + 10
n + 14	n + 15	n + 16	n + 17
n + 21	n + 22	n + 23	n + 24

Activity 52

Word:	HE	HAD	HEAD	HID	HIDE	CHIDE
Set N:	13	13	18	21	26	29
Set S:	89	81	106	161	186	195

BE, BED, BEE, BEG, BEAD or BADE, ACE, FACE, EGG, AID
Remember that most words have at least one vowel.
TAT: Answers will vary

Activity 53

4	2
6	3
5	4
10	3

TAT: Answers will vary.

Activity 54

Network A: two-headed drum
The simplest way to trace each network is to follow the line as far as it goes
before turning.
TAT: 1. 36, square

Activity 55

1. (a) Start or finish at one of the two points at which three line
       segments meet; e.g.: M and N.

J. Weston Walch, Publisher

Activity 55 *(continued)*

2. Consecutive numbers (see table)

Longest Row	Total	Difference
1	1	
2	3	2
3	6	3
4	10	4
5	15	5
6	21	6
7	28	7
8	36	8

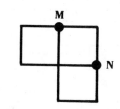

TAT: 2: See answer to 1, a.

Activity 56

Three lines (an odd number) meet at the starting and finishing points. At every other intersection point an even number of lines meet.

TAT: 2. Roads, radio, television, telephone, etc.

Activity 57

TAT: Student discussion

Activity 58

TAT: Student discussion

J. Weston Walch, Publisher